THE REAL McCAIN

*Why Conservatives Don't Trust Him—
and Why Independents Shouldn't*

CLIFF SCHECTER

PoliPointPress

The Real McCain: Why Conservatives Don't Trust
Him—and Why Independents Shouldn't

Copyright © 2008 by Clifford Schecter

Production management: BookMatters
Book design: BookMatters
Cover design: Charles Kreloff

Library of Congress Cataloging-in-Publication
Data has been applied for.

Published by:
POLIPOINTPRESS, LLC
P.O. Box 3008
Sausalito, CA 94966-3008
(415) 339-4100
www.p3books.com

Distributed by Ingram Publisher Services

Printed in the United States of America

To the five people who have meant more to my life than they will ever understand: my late grandfather, Irving "Johnny" Pugatch, who always told me I could do anything; my son Douglas ("Johnny"), who reminds me of this every day; my parents, Phyllis and Keeve, who instilled in me a sense of self and a set of principles that have made me what I am; and most importantly my wife, Anne, whom I love and appreciate more with every passing day.

Contents

ONE

Who Knows McCain?

McCain was not always [a] moderate, tolerant character . . .
He was a conservative before he was a liberal before he
became a conservative again.

Jacob Weisberg, *Slate*

VERO BEACH, FEBRUARY 19, 2007. The senior senator
from Arizona was back in the saddle in pursuit of an office that would make even his four-star admiral forebears
proud. He was in south Florida, but not for the beaches.
He was there to work the evangelical leadership at a private meeting during the National Religious Broadcasters
[NRB] convention. Seems he had a few fences to mend
with the keepers of the Lord's public airwaves. In their
honor, McCain rolled out one of his best signature lines,
the sound bite suited to any occasion for a deft politician:
"What I have found out in my life, is that every time I have
done something for political reasons and not the right reasons, I have paid a heavy price for it—a big price."[1]

No, McCain was not at a convention and trade show in
Florida in February for political reasons, or even for the
weather; he was there for the right reasons (where right

means Right). We are meant to believe he wasn't there for
the same reasons that Sam Brownback, Mitt Romney, and
Duncan Hunter just happened to be there. Nothing political in that. Only righteousness.

Sure, all four happened to be vying for the GOP presidential nomination at the time. They were merely paying calls on the assembled sons of Marconi, Maroni, and
Jesus Christ, whose avowed mission is "to represent the
Christian broadcasters' right to communicate the Gospel
of Jesus Christ to a lost and dying world." Nothing political in addressing such a convention. Even foot soldiers
need a trade organization, it seems, and these God-fearing
communicators with FCC licenses love the truth. In fact,
the NRB's code of ethics includes this quote, supposedly
based on Exodus 20:16: "I will not use the media to know-
ingly speak falsely against anyone."[2]

After his closed-door meeting with God knows who (it
was private, remember), McCain told reporters the substance of his conversation: he emphasized his support for
the war in Iraq, the overturning of *Roe v. Wade*, his opposition to gay marriage, and other concerns that have
stirred his soul and which happen to matter desperately
to the membership of the Lord's media hierarchy here on
earth. To the press later in the day, the Reverend Patrick
Mahoney of the Christian Defense Coalition would ob-
serve that McCain "recognized he cannot be president of
the United States without reaching out to the evangelicals.
He helped himself in that room tremendously today."[3]

If it's not political calculation on McCain's part to tell

the evangelicals what they want to hear, then what is it? This is a man who can tell people that he does nothing for political reasons, and when he does, it gets him in trouble. As the record will show, he has—like Lucy Ricardo—often had plenty of "splainin'" to do about changing his mind on certain issues. But he insists—and for the most part the media is buying it—that he is just caught up in saying what he thinks. He's even made a signature character trait out of it—the straight-talking McCain riding the Straight Talk Express through America.

I bought it once. I gave the man a campaign contribution of twenty dollars back in 2000, when I thought he held informed, principled positions high above the fray of partisan politics. *That* moderate McCain vanished, just as the corruptible earlier McCain (McCain 1.0) quickly vanished in the late 1990s. Who knows what will follow? The evidence amassed in this book reveals that the real McCain's political calculus has never changed. At every moment he's tracking his target like a sophisticated Defense Department homing system. Moving, adjusting, resighting—aiming for the political advantage of one John Sidney McCain III.

It's not so surprising, then, that the McCain who found it expedient to call the Reverend Jerry Falwell and Pat Robertson "agents of intolerance" when he last ran for president would in 2007 go to Florida to kiss and make up with those he had offended—those who turned out in 2000 and 2004 to be the base of two victorious White House runs by George W. Bush. Although the media, once again, was inclined to buy McCain's reasoned tempering of a previously intemperate swipe at Jerry and Pat, the people he was most trying to persuade—evangelical Christians—weren't necessarily buying it. The image of McCain, Man of Principle above Political Gamesmanship, goes down well with devoted "centrists" like David Broder and even manages to charm left-of-center Comedy Central host Jon Stewart. But the good Reverend Mahoney played a lot harder to get, McCain's Florida blandishments notwithstanding. The relationship between McCain and people of faith, Mahoney would tell the Associated Press after the meeting in Vero Beach, remains "uneasy."[4]

John Sidney McCain III is by turns a warmonger and an uber-isolationist; a pro-life stalwart who was pro-choice (at least rhetorically) in 1999; an opponent of President Bush's tax cuts—because "so many of the benefits go to the most fortunate among us"—but now a supporter of making them permanent; and a man who suffered the misery of torture for five years but who voted in February 2008 to allow waterboarding.[5] To understand the phenomenon that is McCain, you must be familiar with his past. Not that his past is obscure or mysterious—it's an open book, as is anyone's who is running for president *the second time*. But what do the brute facts add up to? That's the question that every American of voting age must decide.

The standard story arc for McCain is that of a man on the move ideologically, politically, and personally. As Jacob Weisberg said in *Slate*, there have been three McCains, so far.[6] So many personas might do irreparable harm to other presidential hopefuls, but McCain will be the GOP nominee in 2008.

A conditional friend to conservatives, an appealing maverick to independents, and a noxious Bush apologist to Democrats, McCain is a unique blend of allegiances and enmities unprecedented in American politics. The McCain in evidence in Vero Beach with the holy-rolling broadcasters—at once obliquely mentioning a past transgression (once having done something for political reasons!), claiming to be in possession of a truth about it ("What I have found out in life . . ."), and yet acting again from political motives—is the *real* McCain: clever, calculating, always political. What conservatives misread as disloyalty to the cause isn't that at all; what moderates and independents value as McCain's free thinking isn't that, either.

From the very beginning of his life, John Sidney McCain III had a sense that he didn't fit in but had to. Born August 29, 1936, in the Panama Canal Zone, outside the United States but on U.S. soil (at the time), he began life in a highly regimented military caste. His father (John II) and grandfather (John I) were both admirals in the U.S. Navy. John I commanded the carrier forces in the Pacific during World War II and participated in the Allied triumph in the Battle of Leyte Gulf, considered by many to be the largest sea battle in history, with more than 150,000 combatants. After witnessing the official Japanese surrender on the *USS Missouri* on September 2, 1945, he flew home to California and dropped dead of a heart attack four days later.

McCain's father, like his grandfather, attended the U.S.

Naval Academy; he became a submarine commander and saw lots of action in the Pacific in World War II. John II was credited with sinking two Japanese ships while commander. During the Vietnam War, he occupied the post of commander in chief of the U.S. Pacific Command from 1968 to 1972; his son and namesake was a prisoner of war in Hanoi that whole time.

McCain's father married his mother, Roberta Wright, the daughter of an Oklahoma oil wildcatter, in Cesar's Bar in Tijuana. The lineage in both families wended through Mississippi, where his great-great grandfather, William Alexander McCain, was a slaveholder who fought and died for the Confederacy. Young McCain, known as "Johnny," lived the life familiar to any military kid: you live where your father's postings say you live, whether in Groton, Connecticut, or Pearl Harbor, Hawaii. Eventually, the family settled in northern Virginia when Johnny was about ten, and he wise-guyed his way through the regimented and prestigious Episcopal High School in Alexandria. McCain was pugnacious and a good wrestler.

John Sidney McCain III entered the U.S. Naval Academy at Annapolis—he may have had the choice to go elsewhere, but why would he want to depart from family tradition? His career at the academy was undistinguished in the usual sense—by accomplishment, say—but quite memorable in terms of rebelliousness. He was a proud member of the Century Club, an exclusive group of miscreants who had accumulated a hundred or more demerits. He also boxed for three years on the navy team, where he was less a boxer than a fighter. Of nearly 899 students in the Annapolis class of 1958, only five finished behind McCain III, but few came from his naval pedigree and fewer still have been more successful in life since.

After graduating, McCain trained as a naval aviator in Pensacola, Florida, and in Texas at Corpus Christi. He was a little wild; it was peacetime, after all. Was McCain aimless? Undistinguished? "I generally misused my good health and youth," he later said of those callow years, during which he drove a sports car and dated a lady called Marie the Flame.[7] As an aviator, he struggled with his flying. After surviving two years of flight school—and one test flight crash into Corpus Christi Bay—McCain became a navy pilot.

He was deployed on aircraft carriers in the Caribbean and the Mediterranean. But when the Cold War heated up, McCain found himself on the *USS Enterprise* as part of the blockade of Cuba, ordered by President Kennedy in 1962.

The footloose McCain married Carol Shepp, a Philadelphia model whom he had known back in his Annapolis days. Shepp had married and then divorced a midshipman. McCain adopted Shepp's two children, and in 1966 they had a child together. By 1967, tired of pilot training, McCain requested a combat assignment. His father was now commander in chief of U.S. Naval Forces in Europe. Surely, McCain could have stayed out of combat, but he decided not to.

The story of McCain's being shot down over Hanoi in

October 1967—the injuries suffered in the crash (three limbs broken) and his brutal treatment during five and a half years as a prisoner of war—is well documented. So is his rejection of an offer of release that was due to the McCain family connections. So heroic is the McCain story that even the admissions McCain made to his captors while under duress are forgiven—as they should be. Granted, if McCain were a Democrat and Karl Rove were still on the loose, he might have been "swift-boated" (a reference to unsupported allegations of misdeeds by John Kerry during his Vietnam service) in 2000, when McCain challenged George W. Bush for the Republican presidential nomination. During his captivity, he told French reporters that he was being treated well, he confessed to bombing civilian targets, and he thanked doctors and "the Vietnamese people" for saving his life. Nonetheless, it is worth noting that, on his return, the statements he made while under interrogation did not result in prosecution for violation of the Uniform Code of Military Justice. McCain's name was worth something.

These days, the media has little stomach for swift-boating. The efforts of a group called Vietnam Veterans Against McCain, which in January 2008 accused the "Hanoi Hilton Songbird" of collaborating with the enemy and giving up flight plans and target schedules, went largely unreported.[8] No, McCain's POW heroics are held by almost all segments of the American public and media as proof of the man's courage, principles, and patriotism. Indeed, they are all three. Sadly, they have everything to do with how he is perceived but little to do with what he has become.

Arriving back in the United States in 1973, McCain faced not only his own lingering injuries but also those that his wife had sustained in an automobile accident in 1969. After nine months of intensive physical therapy, he was reinstated to flight status. While stationed in Jacksonville, Florida, he was instrumental in turning around the performance of a Corsair squadron.

His marriage did not recover so well. McCain has admitted to "selfishness and immaturity" and has attributed the breakup of his marriage to his own misdeeds. He has even gone out of his way to exempt Vietnam from any blame. "The blame was entirely mine," he said.[9]

McCain had already met and romanced, while still married to Shepp, the woman who would be his second wife—Cindy Lou Hensley, seventeen years his junior, the only child of a wealthy Anheuser-Busch distributor from Phoenix.[10] Cindy's father, Jim Hensley, had been a World War II pilot, shot down over the English Channel. In 1955 he formed his company, Hensley & Co., now the country's sixth-largest beer distributorship. Cindy had gone from cheerleader to rodeo queen to graduate student at University of South Carolina by the time she met McCain in 1979. A year later, McCain and his first wife were granted a divorce; six weeks later, McCain married Cindy. In 1982 he signed his discharge papers and buried his father in Arlington National Cemetery on the same day. Then he took a job with his new father-in-law's beer company. In the process, he became an Arizonan.

To many questions in life, beer is undoubtedly the right answer, and it was the right answer at the right time for the increasingly ambitious McCain in 1982. As vice-president of public relations at Hensley & Co., McCain inherited business connections that gave him access to wealthy businessmen, including real estate mogul Charles Keating and newspaper publisher Duke Tully. When Republican John Jacob Rhodes announced he was stepping down from the U.S. House of Representatives after serving Arizona's First Congressional District for thirty years, McCain, a war hero with clout in a conservative state, threw his hat in the ring. Assailed by some as a carpetbagger, McCain came up with this devastating refutation at a candidate's forum:

> Listen, pal. I spent twenty-two years in the navy. My father
> was in the navy. My grandfather was in the navy. We in the
> military service tend to move a lot. We have to live in all
> parts of the country, all parts of the world. I wish I could
> have had the luxury, like you, of growing up and living and
> spending my entire life in a nice place like the First District
> of Arizona, but I was doing other things. As a matter of fact,
> when I think about it now, the place I lived longest in my life
> was Hanoi.[11]

For perhaps the first time, McCain had found a political use for his Vietnam experience.

McCain won. A nice loan from his wife helped, as did the endorsement of the *Arizona Republic,* published by his new buddy Duke Tully. As a freshman House member, McCain became involved in an important Arizona issue—Indian affairs. He sponsored several bills having to do with tribal Indian lands and tax status, but resulting legislation was sparse. McCain called himself a foreign policy "realist" and acted on this characterization by favoring a "gradual pullout" from Lebanon after the attack on the Marine barracks in 1983. His stance differed from that of the Reagan White House, but that would sit well with Barry Goldwater, the Arizona senator whose seat McCain coveted.[12] (The neocon McCain would call this position "waving the white flag.") Later, this Vietnam veteran stood up to conservatives in his own party to normalize relations with the country where he had once been a tortured prisoner of war.[13]

In 1986 McCain ran for the Senate seat being vacated by the retiring Goldwater—whose libertarian, noninterventionist, anti–New Deal philosophy was crucial to the formation of McCain 1.0. McCain ran unopposed in the Republican primary; as for Democratic opposition, popular governor Bruce Babbit gave it a look and decided not to go there. McCain easily defeated a man named Richard Kimball and won his first six-year term to the U.S. Senate.

McCain's close connections to business interests came back to haunt him. In November 1991 it was revealed that he had been up to his epaulets in the infamous Keating Five scandal. The charge was that five U.S. senators had received donations for easing regulations on a savings and loan run by Phoenix, Arizona–based tycoon Charles

Keating. In McCain's case, the donations amounted to
$56,000 for his two House races and $54,000 for his 1986
U.S. Senate race, not to mention free use of Keating's corporate jet, paid commercial air travel for McCain and his
family, and vacations in the Bahamas.[14] What did Keating
receive in return, and how did it affect McCain at the
time? According to Mark Levin, writing for the *National
Review Online*:

> [McCain] was investigated by the Senate Select Committee
> on Ethics in 1991 regarding the acceptance of favors from
> Lincoln Savings & Loan Association (Lincoln) and its owner,
> Charles H. Keating, Jr. Simply put, the issue was whether
> McCain and the other senators used their official positions
> to attempt to pressure Federal Home Loan Bank board
> officials to go easy on the troubled institution. Eventually,
> Lincoln went bust, costing depositors and taxpayers
> millions.[15]

Although McCain's actions did not quite merit "institu-
tional action" against him, Levin reports that the committee found that "given the personal benefits and campaign
contributions he had received from Mr. Keating, Senator
McCain instituted 'poor judgment' in intervening with the
regulators without first inquiring as to the bank board's
position in the case in a more routine manner."[16]

When the scandal broke, McCain discarded his opposition to campaign finance reform and became one
of its staunchest proponents. He worked with Wisconsin
Democrat Russ Feingold on a bill meant to put an end to

the soft money that could be cleverly directed to specific campaigns. The rabid fundraisers of the evangelical base would resent McCain's role in this legislation, which took many years to pass.[17]

On most other issues, McCain remained a stalwart Republican in his voting habits. That is, until he decided, in 1999, to run for president in 2000. With George W. Bush and Steve Forbes battling it out for the attentions of the far right, thereby splitting the base of the Republican Party, McCain seemed to spot his best chance as staking out the position of a moderate Republican—McCain 2.0.

Suddenly McCain became the darling of the media. The McCain campaign embraced the notion of "straight talk"—his bus was dubbed the "Straight Talk Express"—and McCain invited reporters on board for informal chats. Soon the media couldn't get enough of the charismatic "maverick." He received loads of free media attention, which is everything an underfinanced underdog could want.

He needed it. Governor George W. Bush of Texas was reeling in more money than the Sultan of Brunei. The media's love affair with McCain made him a danger to Bush, who was busy sledding in New Hampshire and attracting high-powered endorsements on little more than his name and family connections. But in the first presidential primary of the new millennium, McCain shocked the complacent Bushies by earning a nineteen- point victory in the Granite State.

The large and wealthy Bush team reacted. The next primary was in South Carolina, and the Bush camp threw out every over-the-top charge one could imagine. Loose-knit groups affiliated with the Bush campaign or his funding cabal questioned McCain's mental health after his time in the "Hanoi Hilton"; called his wife a drug addict (she did once have a problem with prescription drugs); lied about his political positions (made easier, frankly, by the fact that so many of them had changed during the election season, such as his newfound support for the Confederate flag); and, most despicably, suggested he might have a black "love child," in reference to the Bangladeshi girl he and his wife had adopted.[18] McCain was soundly defeated in the Palmetto State.

Even though he rebounded with a victory in Michigan's primary, the financial, organizational, and family advantages—not to mention the cutthroat politics of the "WASP Corleones"—became too much for McCain to overcome.[19] The predictable result was that George W. Bush—the one-and-a-half-term governor whose greatest accomplishments were running numerous businesses into the ground, beating a befuddled Ann Richards in an election, and duping the good people of Arlington, Texas, into building a new ballpark that would make him a multimillionaire—was given the keys to the White House.

McCain's reaction to the election was characteristically pugnacious. Determined to be a thorn in Bush's side, he took what seemed like courageous stands at the time: opposing Bush tax cuts, cosponsoring a patient's bill of rights with senators Edward Kennedy (D-MA) and John Edwards (D-NC), and reviving his campaign finance reform bill with Russ Feingold. He even got on the environmental bandwagon for a short spin with old friend and fellow veteran John Kerry by proposing legislation to raise average fuel-economy standards. With then-Democrat Joseph Lieberman, he proposed liberal social legislation, including an attempt to close a gun show loophole you could drive a tank through.

Was this a shift in the political philosophy of the good senator from Arizona? Was McCain employing common sense and taking the public good into serious account?

Some high-ranking Republicans believe McCain was motivated simply and purely by revenge on the Bush machine and allied conservatives, which had so mercilessly attacked him in South Carolina. In fact, one long-time conservative activist, Richard Viguerie, started a website in February of 2008 called ConservativeHQ.com to "relaunch the conservative movement."[20] In his debut email promoting the site, he attacked McCain, "who seems to have disdain for conservatives and conservative ideas." This sentiment could often be heard in a growing chorus from the Right starting all the way back in 2001.

But the "changes" in McCain's political persona made some of my Democratic friends and me fall into his camp. We thought McCain might join the Democrats or at least help pass progressive legislation, and I even wrote an article that praised him as a "reformer," and "bipartisan."[21] Sound familiar? McCain 2.0 had snowed me and many other progressives as well as independents.

McCain's pique with the Party of Bush worsened. When Bush turned his back on GOP moderates, longtime Republican James Jeffords of Vermont became an independent and decided to caucus with the Democrats, giving them control of the Senate in 2001. The Democrats tried to convince McCain to join their ranks. The media salivated over his impending switch, especially when Tom Daschle visited McCain's Sedona ranch in May, but the Arizona senator decided to stay put in the GOP. We now know it was McCain who initiated talk of a potential party switch with top Democrats through his longtime political consultant John Weaver.

Having made his choice to stay among the elephants, John McCain rediscovered his inner religious conservative—which had never existed before—and began drifting toward the Creationism wing of his party. He was once again looking for love—or a warm base.

But not for long. In 2004 John Kerry, the Democratic presidential nominee, began floating the idea of a unity ticket, which would include McCain as vice-presidential nominee.[22] At first McCain didn't dismiss the idea, perhaps because it was his. McCain once again had sent John Weaver across the aisle as his emissary. Did McCain use the possible switch as a way to wring concessions out of the Republican hierarchy? That question remains unanswered. In the end McCain rejected "Kerry's offer" and endorsed President Bush for reelection, thereby contradicting many principles he claimed to stand for.

The fully formed neoconservative McCain, the traditionalist and corporatist from the 1980s and most of the 1990s, was reborn. This McCain professed a new mission-ary's zeal for sending in cluster bombs with a wing and a prayer. Call him McCain 3.0.

On the pivotal question of the war in Iraq, McCain began to call for more troops than Rumsfeld wanted to deploy. When more troops were eventually sent in after Rumsfeld's resignation, the violence did decrease. McCain appeared vindicated, even though Iraq was ravaged and the U.S. mission there grew ever murkier and open-ended with no political solution in sight.

The newest McCain is also staunchly anti-choice and has called for a constitutional amendment to ban abor-tion. Everyone should simply forget what he said in 1999 about not wanting to overturn *Roe v. Wade*.[23] That was McCain 2.0 speaking. This man who met with the Log Cabin Republicans—a gay group working to promote ac-ceptance of gays within their party—and who opposed a federal amendment banning gay marriage now wanted to ban gay marriage in Arizona. (That measure lost.) McCain 3.0 no longer sees Jerry Falwell as intolerant. Swift Boaters did some good work, despite having heaped a payload of horse manure on the war record of McCain's friend (and near running mate!) John Kerry. In fact, McCain 3.0 likes them so much that he has accepted funding from the sul-tans of sleaze for his presidential bid.

As the 2008 election unfolds, we will see which long-held beliefs McCain retains in the scramble toward the top. Can he afford to be principled on campaign reform?

How will he feel about the conservative base of the party, which he is courting so energetically? Will he accept its choice for vice president and promise to appoint judges to overturn *Roe v. Wade?* Or is a tough stance on immigration his new bargaining chip? Will he pledge never to raise taxes? How about outlawing the IRS or banishing the estate tax forever?

Late in the summer of 2007, McCain was down in the polls, nearly out of money, and still backing a very unpopular war and president. But by year's end his decision to recommend more troops in Iraq and the lull in lethal violence there had infused McCain with a new credibility. His campaign caught on. The media—Imus, Tim Russert, Broder, each of them "my friend," in McCain's parlance—remained there for him. He is now the Republican frontrunner. He is now no longer the thorn in the Bush's side, but the man standing next to the Bushes as they give their endorsements.

The tough McCain is coming: the tough-minded, tough-to-read, sharp-tongued, tough-to-take, cantankerous, charming, and always winning maverick is coming to a living room near you. True, he was once—inarguably!—a principled man, a hero who served our country with honor and valor. And that makes him hard to resist. Harder still if we ignore evidence of his reversals, shady dealings, arrogant attacks on those who stand in his way, and stunning betrayals of those who were loyal to him or with whom he shared a life experience.

As is well known, the conservatives in this country don't

trust this McCain; they don't believe that the real McCain is a real conservative. They are hesitant to put their money and clout behind a man who might not appoint judge after judge with a pro-life stance. They would never wish to boost the career of a man who might raise taxes in a budgetary crunch or believe that the climate crisis is real. The conservatives acutely sense that this man's notion of what is right, or Right, in the world differs from their own.

Democrats might be wise to fear that this skepticism on the Right will translate into an unwitting endorsement, making McCain acceptable to independents—people who just might be attracted to a candidate who is beloved by neither organized party, a maverick and a free thinker, like themselves.

The chapters that follow show how the Real McCain has operated—as reflected in his seemingly unfathomable congressional record; his changeable attitude toward war and intervention; his waffling on campaign finance reform; and his flexible take on ethics, social issues, torture, and taxes. This book is more than a cautionary tale. It's enough to make you vote for someone else. I want my twenty bucks back.

TWO

McCain Has Left the Building

Whenever we see anyone wearing their flip-flops, we say,
"I see you have your McCains on today."

High-ranking Senate staffer

WHEN JOHN MCCAIN WAS ELECTED to the U.S. Senate in 1986 (after four years in the House), voters thought they had chosen someone who would conduct himself in a characteristically maverick Arizona fashion. Once a Confederate territory, Arizona became the last of the contiguous states to join the Union. McCain, a man with a country but no particular place called home, brought his war record, the impressive McCain military pedigree, and a new bride with local connections to a place that seemed tailor-made for him—a place of abundant opportunity and short tradition, where a man with the right smarts and access to some capital could make himself part of the Arizona story.

During his two terms representing Arizona's First District in the House of Representatives (1983–1986), McCain showed glimmers of being a worthy successor to the beloved Barry Goldwater, whose brand of conservatism—populist,

anti-Communist, and isolationist—had made a considerable impact on the Republican Party. McCain went against
President Reagan on troop deployment in Lebanon; he
crossed him again when voting to override a presidential
veto of a bill sanctioning South Africa for its apartheid
policies. When the fifty-year-old McCain took the retiring
Goldwater's seat in the Senate, he was thought to be just
the man to represent the state's unique character. But such
expectations were not to be met on the home front.

In many ways, McCain has been a spectator on the
Senate scene. He watched the Republican Party reinvent
itself with Ronald Reagan rather than Barry Goldwater
as its presiding spirit. He largely went with the flow while
Republican activists like Newt Gingrich moved the party
farther to the right and forged a fateful alliance with an
evangelical religious base. Goldwater, who fought the influence of the Christian right on abortion and school prayer,
voiced his displeasure before he passed away: "Every good
Christian ought to kick Jerry Falwell right in the ass. I get
damn tired of those political preachers telling me what I
ought to believe in and do."[1] McCain became estranged
from the dominant strain of the party and was humiliated
by the party's dirty tricks in the 2000 South Carolina primary. The ascendant Bushes, who inherited the Reagan
mantle, thrashed him like an apostate—or a Democrat.
After his defeat, McCain would make them think they
weren't far off the mark.

To be sure, McCain has had his legislative moments,

as when he sponsored the much-ballyhooed campaign finance reform bill. Indeed, if McCain's maverick reputation is based on anything of true substance, it is the campaign finance reform he pushed so hard in the wake of an early career blunder. It was convenient for McCain to become a reformer on the heels of his entanglement in the Charles Keating S&L scandal. Having been identified as one of the Keating Five, he cosponsored a bill with Wisconsin Democrat Russ Feingold to exorcise the demons of corruption.[2] The McCain-Feingold-Cochran Campaign Reform Bill—which became the Bipartisan Campaign Reform Act—was intended to address the growing influence of soft money in the electoral process and to confront the problem of "issue ads" run by 527 groups. These groups are named for a section of the tax code that allows them to influence the outcome of an election without submitting to regulation by the Federal Election Commission or state agencies and without adhering to contribution limits placed on political action committees (PACs).

The McCain-Feingold legislation finally became law in January 2003, nine years after it was proposed and fourteen years after the S&L fraud for which Keating was convicted—and from which thousands of investors never recovered. But McCain recovered: he managed to get the very bankable term *reformer* attached to his name.[3] Although it appears McCain was merely attempting to put the dogs off the hunt of his shady dealings, he had stumbled onto his signature issue.

In fairness, McCain-Feingold is not all McCain has done in the Senate. In 1994 he worked with Democrat John Kerry on behalf of legislation calling for the fullest possible accounting of American servicemen unaccounted for during the war in Vietnam, and he encouraged the president to lift the U.S. trade embargo against Vietnam. In 1995 President Bill Clinton announced the normalization of diplomatic relations with Vietnam over the protests of a dwindling band of MIA activists. McCain deserves credit for helping to put Vietnam behind us.

Campaign finance reform legislation and normalization of U.S.-Vietnam relations are virtually the only instances in which McCain has distinguished himself as a Senate leader. And McCain appears to be backing away from campaign finance reform. Nevertheless, the label *maverick* sticks to him like white on rice.

MEDIA DARLING

When the media assigns an identity—accurately or inaccurately—to a politician, that identity often becomes the prevailing conventional wisdom. McCain is now permanently marked as a straight talker. And who is he talking straight to? The media. "The press loves McCain," said MSNBC's Chris Matthews in September 2006. "We're his base."[4]

McCain knows how to work his base—by joshing, flirting, and being unguarded and obstreperous with a bevy of reporters whose job is to work the McCain beat. By the spring of 2008 McCain had perfected his tactics, as Ryan

Lizza's *New Yorker* piece, "On the Bus," amply demonstrated. "McCain has been doing a version of the Straight Talk show for so long the veterans know all the lines," writes Lizza. He reports that McCain tells a newbie, "A condition of entry . . . [is] sarcasm, lack of sincerity," to which a chief aide adds, "and a willingness to laugh at the same jokes."[5]

McCain's appearances on talk shows often have that same feel of a commander drinking with his men but controlling the bottle—McCain heaving in stiffly with his tight grin, mixing policy talk with banter. Jon Stewart, Tim Russert, Don Imus—they all act as if the candidate on their show is doing them a favor. The straight-talking maverick, the outside-the-beltway interloper, is the consummate politician, moving the media pieces around the board. He wants them in his war.

With all due respect to the war hero McCain, let's take a closer look at the man who would be president. Not the man who gritted his way through five-plus years of horror in Hanoi, but the man who has spent two and a half cushy decades in Congress without very much to show for it. For a man with a reputation as a straight shooter, McCain's actions as a senator reveal him to be an extraordinarily opportunistic politician.

ABSENT FROM DUTY

Unlike George W. Bush, McCain could never be accused of being AWOL from the military. But an examination of his congressional voting record might earn him the tag AWOC, or "Absent Without Courage." For McCain has shown that when it comes to the tough votes, the ones requiring him to take a stand, he adheres to the ancient philosophy espoused by Mr. Miyagi from *The Karate Kid*: "Best defense, no be there."

Simply put, in the first session of the 110th Congress (2007), the senator from Arizona missed, by a wide margin, more votes than any of his Senate colleagues but one, Democrat Tim Johnson, who was sidelined with a serious brain hemorrhage.[6]

According to the *Washington Post* database tracking Senate "vote missers," McCain had missed a whopping 261 of 468 votes, or almost 56 percent, by March 2008. McCain is understandably busy running for president—and all the candidates running for that highest of offices in 2008 have shown a poor record in showing up for votes. But number of votes missed is one thing; *which* votes you miss is another. McCain the maverick has missed votes in a way that betrays a calculated strategy: namely, to avoid going on the record when doing so would be politically risky.

On March 13, 2007, a critical roll call vote was held in the Senate on the Improving America's Security Act, which codified implementation of the 9/11 Commission recommendations for protecting America. Barack Obama and Hillary Clinton were there. So were then–presidential candidates senators Chris Dodd of Connecticut, Joe Biden of Delaware, and Sam Brownback of Kansas. Where was

John McCain? According to his official calendar, he was in California for a series of big-money fundraisers.

Did Arizona's senior senator think a key vote on *protecting America* wasn't important enough to make? Could it be that McCain didn't want to go against the wishes of his party and be on the record—with thirty-eight other Republicans—in opposing increased security for America? McCain was the only senator, other than Tim Johnson, to miss that vote.[7]

McCain wasn't out of town on the presidential campaign trail but was instead practicing the art of selective voting—the art of "no be there"—on March 23. It was a busy legislative day that saw sixteen roll call votes on the floor. McCain voted dependably, right down the party line, on fifteen of those proposed votes. One might surmise that the missed vote occurred early in the morning, before McCain got to the office, or late at night, after he'd left, maybe to attend a fundraiser or get a beer with Imus.

Wrong. The vote McCain missed that day occurred right in the middle of the legislative day and between two other votes for which he was present. The one he missed was for an amendment (Amdt. 529) to provide $1.2 billion for the highly successful COPS program, an initiative that gives "local law enforcement critical resources necessary to prevent and respond to violent crime and acts of terrorism." Perhaps the issues before and after the ducked vote were not as uncomfortable for McCain. Have a look at the vote timeline for the hour in question:

Vote	Issue	Time of Vote	McCain Vote
109	DeMint Amdt. No. 578; To repeal the death tax	1:13 PM	Yes
110	Biden Amdt. No. 529; To increase funding for the COPS Program to $1.15 billion for FY 2008 to provide state and local law enforcement with critical resources necessary to prevent and respond to violent crime and acts of terrorism and is offset by an unallocated reduction to non-defense discretionary spending and/or reduction to administrative expenses.	1:32 PM	Not Voting
111	Bunning Amdt. No. 594 as Modified; To provide a deficit-neutral reserve fund for protecting State flexibility in Medicaid.	1:52 PM	Yes

It's possible that Senator McCain just happened to be in the men's room or the Senate cafeteria when vote number 110 was held. Or maybe he didn't want to be on record as voting against a provision called the Improving America's Security Act. McCain, unlike his thirty-three colleagues, would have to stand by that vote as a presidential candidate in 2008.

McCain found a way to miss most of the important votes on Iraq in the first part of the 110th Congress. He even bailed on a critical Iraq war briefing by General David

Petraeus on April 25, 2007, so that he could campaign in New Hampshire that day.[8]

Yet his speeches suggest complete vigilance. "We must win in Iraq. We cannot fail," said McCain in a May 2006 speech to the Utah State Republican Convention.[9] "If we lose in Iraq, they're coming after us. We will fight them somewhere else—like here. It's all part of a gigantic, titanic struggle between good and evil."[10] Senate Majority Leader Harry Reid took notice: "Senator McCain," Reid said through his spokesperson Liz Oxhorn in May 2007, "has spent considerable time defending the president on Iraq . . . but has only managed to show up for four of the last fourteen Iraq votes."[11]

FRIEND OF THE WORKING FAMILY?

When McCain does cast a vote, it's usually not a progressive one.

Let's start with low-wage workers. If you're among the millions of Americans who work hard, play by the rules, and earn minimum wage, John McCain is not your friend. McCain has voted against every initiative to raise the federal minimum wage since it was last raised in 1997.

In late 2006 the federal minimum wage set a new record for the longest period without a raise since its establishment in 1938. As of December 2, 2006, the $5.15-per-hour wage rate had remained unchanged for nine years and three months. When Democrats took over the Congress in 2007, McCain fought a minimum wage increase until it was tied to more generous tax breaks for business. Before that compromise vote, McCain had voted against raising the rate six times.

McCain did step up to the plate to vote affirmatively on a January 2007 bill by troglodyte Wayne Allard (R-CO), a bill that would have killed the federal minimum wage entirely and returned all control to the states. To give you an idea of how much fun that would be for workers, Kansas has a state-mandated minimum wage of $2.70 per hour. That bill finally caused the cordial Ted Kennedy (D-MA) to call out McCain and his Republican cronies on the Senate floor.

> What is the price, we ask the other side? What is the price that you want from these working men and women? What cost? How much more do we have to give to the private sector and to business? How many billion dollars more, are you asking, are you requiring? When does the greed stop, we ask the other side? That's the question and that's the issue.
>
> What is it about it that drives you Republicans crazy? What is it? What is the price that the workers have to pay to get an increase? What is it about working men and women that you find so offensive?[12]

McCain also voted for the hideous bankruptcy bill in March 2005. This bill was a gift to the banks and finance companies. It made it virtually impossible for working Americans who suffer serious financial setbacks due to catastrophic illness or other involuntary events to file for traditional bankruptcy—thus ensuring their perpetual servitude to the credit card companies.

The Action Council of the Children's Defense Fund named McCain "America's Worst Senator for Children."[13] Among his heartless votes was his opposition to reauthorization of the State Children's Health Insurance Program (SCHIP) in August 2007. The bill would have provided health care to 3.2 million kids whose families have too much income for Medicaid but can't afford health insurance.[14]

KEEPING AMERICA SAFE?

The illusion of John McCain as the great defender of our security and our fighting men and women has grown thinner than Rudy Giuliani's old comb-over.

In the run-up to the 2006 midterm election campaign, the GOP spin machine lied when they said that Democrats had "no plan" for national security. In truth, Biden and countless others had plans aplenty. To provide cover for the bogus claim, the Senate's GOP leadership, including McCain, killed the Real Security Act of 2006—a national-security blueprint proposed by Democrats—on September 13, 2006. Only at that point was the claim that the Democrats had no plan true.

A look at the votes that took place in 2005 and 2006 shows that McCain never wavered in voting against every idea the Democrats put forth to make America safer from emerging threats.

Senator Debbie Stabenow (D-MI) introduced several

bills that would have provided critical funds for equipment that allows emergency first-responders to effectively communicate with one another during natural disasters, terrorist attacks, and other public safety emergencies. Stabenow, who was the driving force behind first-responder legislation in the 109th Congress, worked hard to overcome the McCain-GOP blockade in the Senate:

- Senate Amendment (S. Amdt.) 147: To protect the American people from terrorist attacks by providing the necessary resources to our firefighters, police, EMS workers, and other first-responders by restoring $1,626 billion in cuts to first-responder programs. *(March 15, 2005)*

- S. Amdt. 1217: To provide funding for interoperable communications equipment grants. *(July 14, 2005)*

- S. Amdt. 1687: To provide funding for interoperable communications equipment grants. *(September 14, 2005)*

- S. Amdt. 3056: To provide $5 billion for our emergency responders so that they can field effective and reliable interoperable communications equipment to respond to natural disasters, terrorist attacks, and the public safety needs of America's communities. *(March 15, 2006)*

McCain voted against all of these amendments because the money to help first responders would come from closing tax loopholes.

Senator Charles Schumer (D-NY) also tried to bolster America's national security. Schumer's primary concerns were the transport of hazardous materials and cargo inspection, a rational concern for any New Yorker. In July 2006 McCain voted against Schumer's S. Amdt. 4587, which sought to increase the amount appropriated for transit security by $300 million.

McCain also voted to kill S. Amdt. 4930, proposed by Schumer and other Senate Democrats, to improve maritime container security by "ensuring that foreign ports participating in the Container Security Initiative scan all containers shipped to the United States for nuclear and radiological weapons before loading."

McCain didn't show up for a March 2007 vote on Schumer's S. Amdt. 298, another measure to strengthen the security of cargo. Perhaps McCain thought this measure had a prayer of passing, and he didn't want to be on record as being against it. The measure did pass.

Senator Robert Menendez (D-NJ) championed port security in 2006, as anyone from New Jersey should, given the tremendous exposure the Garden State has in that area. Menendez tried and failed to have two measures passed in 2006: S. Amdt. 3054 would have provided an additional $965 million (fully offset through the closure of tax loopholes) to make U.S. ports more secure by increasing port security grants, increasing inspections, and improving existing programs; and S. Amdt. 4999 would have improved the security of cargo containers destined for the United States. McCain voted against both amendments.

He also voted against America's firefighters when he said no to S. Amdt. 4641 in July 2006. Proposed by Senator

Christopher Dodd (D-CT), the amendment was "to fund urgent priorities for our nation's firefighters, law enforcement personnel, [and] emergency medical personnel." It died on the Senate floor because Dodd suggested paying for the priorities "by reducing the tax breaks for individuals with annual incomes in excess of $1,000,000"—obviously the kiss of death in a GOP-controlled Congress. Carrying firefighters on the backs of the rich? No can do, said McCain's vote.

The common thread through all of these "just say no" to bolstering-national-security amendments was that McCain, the alleged maverick, was doing exactly what his party bosses told him to do. To the Republicans, it would seem, money spent in the predominantly Democratic East Coast port cities was money misspent.

Also consider that these votes weren't procedural devices that allowed McCain to vote for Republican bills with similar, noble intent. After voting against many such bills that tried to bolster homeland security and that had no Republican alternatives, McCain has yet to offer any substantive legislation to strengthen America.

SUPPORTER OF TROOPS AND VETERANS?

Maybe McCain really doesn't believe in homeland security as much as he does in showing force abroad. Maybe he's less interested in saving firefighters and cargo workers than he is in fighting men and women. You would think that as a war hero, he'd be an ace on military and veterans issues. But a look at merely two years' worth of those votes would tempt even the most charitable person to wonder what Senator McCain has against our troops.

As Democrats toiled in 2005 and 2006 to help defend the homeland, they did their best to take care of our troops and veterans. Leading the charge were senators Dodd, Daniel Akaka, Barbara Boxer, Patty Murray, and John Kerry. Unfortunately, they ran into John McCain and the GOP naysayers in the majority, who blocked their attempts at every turn.

Many good deeds died on the vine under John McCain and the 109th Congress's Republican leadership.

- In 2005 Senator Daniel Akaka (D-HI), now chairman of the Senate Veterans' Affairs Committee, introduced S. Amdt. 149, in which he sought to increase veterans' medical care by $2.8 billion in 2006, and S. Amdt. 1852, which would have set aside $10 million for "readjustment counseling services" for those returning from Iraq and Afghanistan. In 2006 Akaka requested $1.5 billion for veterans' medical care and an additional $430 million for the Department of Veteran Affairs for outpatient care and treatment for veterans. John McCain voted against these proposals, while offering no measures of his own and without pushing his party to help America's veterans.

- Senator Dodd's S. Amdt. 2735 proposed additional funding to shore up the failing infrastructures at veterans hospitals all over the country. The bill would have mandated a minor rollback in the capital gains tax cuts that the Bush administration has given to the richest one-fifth of 1 percent of Americans. Dodd proposed the amendment in early 2006. The story of horrors at Walter Reed Hospital broke in February 2007 in an exposé by the *Washington Post.*[15]

• Senator Kerry introduced two pieces of legislation in 2006 to help the troops and America's veterans. In June 2006 Kerry and Senator Russ Feingold (D-WI) authored S. Amdt. 4442 "to require the redeployment of United States Armed Forces from Iraq in order to further a political solution in Iraq, encourage the people of Iraq to provide for their own security, and achieve victory in the war on terror." It got thirteen votes. Needless to say, McCain's vote wasn't one of those thirteen.

• In 2005 Senator Barbara Boxer (D-CA) saw her S. Amdt. 2634 killed, as did Senator Patty Murray (D-WA) with her S. Amdt. 344. These amendments would have funded additional medical care and readjustment counseling for Iraq veterans with mental illness, post-traumatic stress disorder, or substance use disorder. McCain voted no on both.

• Stabenow stepped up for veterans, as she did for emergency responders, by proposing legislation in 2005 and again in 2006 that would have indexed veterans' health care benefits to take into account the annual changes in the veteran's population and inflation. She proposed paying for the indexing by restoring the pre-2001 top tax rate for income over $1 million, closing corporate tax loopholes, and delaying tax cuts for the wealthy. You can guess how this one turned out.

- In February 2006 Jack Reed (D-RI) sponsored S. Amdt. 2737, which would have rolled back capital gains tax cuts so that much-needed equipment for troops serving in Iraq and Afghanistan could be purchased. McCain and the Republican leadership made sure those tax cuts stayed in place, and the troops didn't get what they needed.

Senate Democrats made other attempts to help active members of the military and veterans. Senator Dick Durbin (D-IL) even authored legislation that would have exempted military personnel from some facets of the GOP's hideous 2005 bankruptcy bill by disallowing "certain claims by lenders charging usurious interest rates to service members," and by allowing "service members to exempt property based on the law of the State of their premilitary residence." Unbelievably, McCain didn't think people serving in Iraq and Afghanistan should be shielded from *that* law.

Of the cosponsors listed on two measures that members of both parties should be able to embrace, John McCain is noticeably absent. The Homes for Heroes Act, which Senator Obama introduced in April 2007, would help provide housing for low-income veterans and at least begin to solve the problem of homelessness among America's military veterans. The Post-9/11 Veterans Educational Assistance Act of 2007, introduced by freshman Senator Jim Webb (D-VA) in the first week of the 110th Congress, essentially restores the old G.I. Bill and provides returning troops with the more robust educational benefits enjoyed by the men and women who served in the three decades following World War II. "As a veteran who hails from a family with a long history of military service, I am proud to offer this bill as my first piece of legislation in the United States Senate," said Webb, when he introduced his bill in January 2007.[16]

The Iraq and Afghanistan Veterans of America (IAVA), the country's first and largest Iraq veterans group, has made McCain's nonsupport of and lip service to America's active military and veterans much easier to identify. In 2006 IAVA released its report on the members of Congress who truly support American troops, and those who don't. It examined 155 Senate votes since September 11, 2001, on legislation that "affected troops, veterans, or military families" and awarded each senator a grade by comparing his or her votes to the organization's view of what constitutes true support for active troops, veterans, and their families. For anyone who has watched Senate Republicans vote time and time again against legislation that would benefit military families, the results were not shocking.

IAVA gave no senator an A grade. Thirteen senators, all Democrats, received an A-. Of twenty-three senators given a B+, twenty-two were Democrats. The other B+ recipient was Vermont's James Jeffords, an independent who caucused with the Democrats before retiring in 2006.

The worst grade received by a Senate Democrat was higher than the best grade granted to a Republican.

How did IAVA grade John McCain, the guy who everyone thinks of as Mr. Defense and Mr. Support the Troops? He got a D.

This party-line voting pattern suggests that John McCain is a legislative follower—when he shows up at all. The Arizona senator summed it up for us himself in a 2006 *Washington Post* column by David Ignatius. McCain described his loyalty to George W. Bush as being so profound that he wouldn't rule out giving up his Senate seat to become secretary of defense if and when Donald Rumsfeld were to leave. "I would have to assess where I can be most effective," said McCain. "It's awfully hard to say no to the president of the United States."[17]

Yes, your record makes that abundantly clear.

THREE

McCain and Abel

"The thought of his being president sends a cold chill down my spine," Cochran said about McCain by phone. "He is erratic. He is hotheaded. He loses his temper and he worries me."

Republican Senator Thad Cochran of Mississippi, as quoted in the *Boston Globe*, January 27, 2008

ONCE UPON A TIME, LONG, LONG AGO, John McCain called a famous man of God an "agent of intolerance."[1]

Okay, it was Jerry Falwell, it was eight years ago, and no one has let McCain forget it. But with the Lord as his witness, McCain is trying to make up for it. In 2006, as McCain began laying the groundwork for another run at the White House, he sought to shore up his conservative credentials by going to Falwell's Liberty University to beg forgiveness.

It was no secret that Falwell and his religious warriors were McCain's adversaries in the 2000 presidential primary season. But McCain appeared on *Larry King Live* in 2006, proclaiming his loyalty to the very same people. "I admire the Religious Right for the dedication and zeal they put into the political process," he told King.[2] That dedication and zeal had once led Falwell to utter:

These perverted homosexuals . . . absolutely hate everything
that you and I and most decent God-fearing people stand
for . . . Make no mistake. These deviants seek nothing less
than total control and influence in society, politics, our
schools, and in our exercise of free speech and religion.
If we do not act now, homosexuals will control America![3]

Maybe McCain wouldn't say amen to that. Maybe he
simply respects everyone's right to fulminate against same-
sex activity. But after McCain himself became the target
of overzealous campaign rhetoric, the question becomes
a different one. How could McCain cozy up to the Bush
advocates who viciously attacked him and his family in
2000?

Even cynical political operatives were shocked by the
slime the Bush campaign threw at McCain after he won the
2000 New Hampshire primary, and many analysts believed
that a subsequent McCain victory in South Carolina would
have provided him with overwhelming momentum. It was
obvious that the Karl Rove smear machine would shift into
high gear to keep that from happening. And it did.

The South Carolina primary introduced most of the
country to the political tactic of "push polling." The Bush
camp called Republican voters and asked, "Would you be
more likely or less likely to vote for John McCain for president if you knew he had fathered an illegitimate black child?"
The race-baiting was disgusting. But the use of McCain's
daughter Bridget—whom he and his wife had adopted
from Mother Teresa's orphanage in Bangladesh—because

they thought her dark skin might fool the locals flabber-gasted even hardened political pros.[4]

Other indignities the Bush crew heaped on McCain have become the stuff of political lore. Leaflets described McCain as "pro-abortion" and, because he met with the Log Cabin Republicans, "the fag candidate." Rumors circulated that McCain's wife was a "drug addict" due to a problem she once had with prescription painkillers.[5] The Bush advocates even impugned McCain's courage and patriotism and implied that the decorated war hero was mentally unstable because of the time he spent in captivity.[6] Ted Sampley—who later participated in the Swift Boat attacks on John Kerry—compared McCain to "the Manchurian Candidate." He also suggested that McCain had escaped death while in captivity by collaborating with the enemy.[7]

McCain's response to these attacks was remarkably restrained. In a debate before the South Carolina primary, McCain told Bush that he "should be ashamed" for the false and deeply personal attacks.[8] But when Bush received the nomination, McCain worked his heart out on Bush's behalf and embraced him literally and figuratively. He also said that helping Bush win reelection in 2004 was "one of the proudest moments of my life."[9]

One can understand why McCain would choose to turn the other cheek, if only out of political expediency. And in the end, his dignity is his alone to squander. But the choice is quite different when a colleague is similarly smeared. McCain's response to the now-famous swift-boating of his longtime friend John Kerry in 2004 was scarcely more than a whimper of protest. McCain was heard to comment that the Swift Boat campaign was "dishonest and dishonorable," but he did nothing within the Republican Party to end the vicious attacks on a fellow war veteran.[10] Former U.S. Senator Max Cleland, another war hero, delivered a letter to Bush's Crawford ranch at the height of the campaign demanding that Bush "recognize this blatant attempt at character assassination, and publicly condemn it."[11] The letter was signed by seven senators who had served in the military—but not by McCain, who was scheduled to campaign with Bush the following week. Later, McCain gave a rousing speech for Bush at the Republican convention.

Despite McCain's acquiescence to these attacks, he hadn't lost his appetite for a quarrel. The political world was atwitter in early 2006 over a dust-up between Senator Barack Obama and McCain after some sharp exchanges over lobbying reform. After Obama wrote a formal letter asking McCain to support the Honest Leadership Act proposed by the Democrats, McCain's own formal letter to Obama was remarkably peevish. "I would like to apologize to you," he wrote, "for assuming that your private assurances to me regarding your desire to cooperate in our efforts to negotiate bipartisan lobbying reform legislation were sincere." He went on:

> I'm embarrassed to admit that after all these years in politics
> I failed to interpret your previous assurances as typical
> rhetorical gloss routinely used in politics to make self-
> interested partisan posturing appear more noble. Again,

sorry for the confusion, but please be assured I won't make the same mistake again.[12]

McCain then appeared on MSNBC's *Hardball* and told host Chris Matthews that he gave Obama "a little straight talk."[13] McCain may have been testy over routine political maneuvering by Obama, but he had no problem rolling over for the Bush campaign even after it slimed him and his colleagues.

The exchange with Obama raised another question about McCain: could he keep his famous temper? He told an audience in central Michigan, "I'm going to raise the level of political dialogue in America, and I'm going to treat my opponents with respect and demand that they treat me with respect." He has also said, "Legitimate policy differences, those should be debated and discussed. But I don't think you should take shots at people."[14]

But the record doesn't match the rhetoric. In a January 2007 piece for Salon.com, Sidney Blumenthal took a hard look at how McCain is perceived among those who work with him in Washington DC:

> McCain's political colleagues, however, know this McCain
> well—a volatile man with a hair-trigger temper, who shouted
> at Sen. Ted Kennedy on the Senate floor to "shut up," called
> his fellow Republican senators "shithead," "fucking jerk,"
> "asshole," and joked in 1998 at a Republican fundraiser
> about the teenage daughter of President Clinton, "Do you
> know why Chelsea Clinton is so ugly? Because Janet Reno
> is her father." As recently as a few months ago, McCain

suddenly rushed up to a friend of mine, a prominent
Washington attorney, at a social event, and threatened
to beat him up because he represented a client McCain
happened to dislike, and then, just as suddenly, profusely
and tearfully apologized.[15]

In May 2007, McCain made a rare appearance in the nation's capitol to meet with his Republican colleagues on a
possible immigration-bill compromise and got into a nasty
exchange with fellow Republican John Cornyn of Texas.
The shouting match began when Cornyn called McCain
on his late entry into the process. Paul Kane reported the
incident on Capitol Briefing Blog for the *Washington Post*:

> Things got really heated when Cornyn accused McCain of
> being too busy campaigning for president to take part in the
> negotiations, which have gone on for months behind closed
> doors. "Wait a second here," Cornyn said to McCain. "I've
> been sitting in here for all of these negotiations and you just
> parachute in here on the last day. You're out of line."
>
> McCain, a former Navy pilot, then used language more
> accustomed to sailors (not to mention the current vice
> president, who made news a few years back after a verbal
> encounter with Sen. Patrick Leahy of Vermont).
>
> "[Expletive] you! I know more about this than anyone
> else in the room," shouted McCain at Cornyn.[16]

In a *Los Angeles Times* article about the blowup with
Cornyn, David Keene, chairman of the American Conservative Union, said, "In McCain's world, there aren't
legitimate differences of opinions. There is his way and

there is evil. That is how he approaches issues. That is one of the reasons for conservative nervousness about him."

The best McCain campaign spokesman Danny Diaz could muster in response was, "There was a spirited exchange."[17]

A 2006 article for the conservative online magazine *Newsmax* provided accounts from witnesses of other "spirited" exchanges involving McCain.[18] One is former Senator Bob Smith, a New Hampshire Republican who served with McCain on the Senate Armed Services Committee and on Republican policy committees. Smith reported, "He would disagree about something and then explode. [They were] incidents of irrational behavior. We've all had incidents where we have gotten angry, but I've never seen anyone act like that."

The *Newsmax* piece included a former Senate staffer's recollection of what happened when McCain asked for support from a fellow Republican senator on the Commerce, Science, and Transportation Committee. "The senator explained that he had already committed to support George Bush," the former Senate staffer said. "McCain said 'f— you' and never spoke to him again."

Another former senator, who according to the *Newsmax* article requested anonymity, recalled an exchange at a Republican policy lunch in which another senator disagreed with McCain. "McCain used the f-word," the former senator said. "McCain called the guy a 'sh—head.' The senator demanded an apology. McCain stood up and said, 'I apologize, but you're still a sh—head.' That was in front of 40 to 50 Republican senators. That sort of thing happened frequently."

Another witness in the *Newsmax* article is former Representative John LeBoutillier, a New York Republican who had an encounter with McCain when he was on a POW task force in the House. "People who disagree with him get the f— you," said LeBoutillier. "He is a vicious person." He went on to say that when McCain and Bush were vying for the Republican nomination, "Nearly all the Republican senators endorsed Bush because they knew McCain from serving with him in the Senate. They so disliked him that they wouldn't support him. They have been on the hard end of his behavior."

McCain's Senate colleagues have frequently been on the receiving end of his sweet nothings. "Only an asshole would put together a budget like this," he told Budget Committee Chairman and Republican Senator Pete Domenici in 1999. After McCain called Senator Chuck Grassley "a f——jerk" to his face, Grassley refused to speak to him for years.[19]

McCain even had a confrontation with the Senate's oldest member. Strom Thurmond, who ran for president in 1948, probably hadn't been in possession of all his faculties since the days he was fighting for separate water fountains. But even he wasn't safe from McCain's temper.

In January 1995, McCain was midway through an opening statement at a Senate Armed Services Committee hearing when chairman Strom Thurmond asked, 'Is the senator about through?' McCain glared at Thurmond, thanked·him for his 'courtesy' (translation: buzz off), and continued on. McCain later confronted Thurmond on the Senate floor. A scuffle ensued, and the two didn't part friends."[20]

Perhaps the most remarkable story of McCain's temper involved Arizona Congressman Rick Renzi. Two former reporters covering McCain, one who witnessed the following events and one who confirmed the facts provided by the first, relayed it to me as follows: In 2006, the Arizona Republican congressional delegation had a strategy meeting. McCain repeatedly addressed two new members, congressmen Trent Franks and Rick Renzi, as "boy." Finally, Renzi, a former college linebacker, rose from his chair and said to McCain, "You call me that one more time and I'll kick your old ass." McCain lunged at Renzi, punches were thrown, and the two had to be physically separated. After they went to their separate offices, McCain called Renzi and demanded an apology. Renzi refused. Apparently this posture made McCain admire him, as they became fast friends.

Three reporters from Arizona, on the condition of anonymity, also let me in on another incident involving McCain's intemperateness. In his 1992 Senate bid, McCain was joined on the campaign trail by his wife, Cindy, as well as campaign aide Doug Cole and consultant Wes Gullett. At one point, Cindy playfully twirled McCain's hair and said, "You're getting a little thin up there." McCain's face reddened, and he responded, "At least I don't plaster on the makeup like a trollop, you cunt." McCain's excuse was that it had been a long day. If elected president of the United States, McCain would have many long days.

What should voters make of this pattern? In February 2008 Tim Russert succinctly described McCain on MSNBC's *Morning Joe*. A devilish grin spread from ear to ear as Russert, no McCain hater, leaned forward and spoke in a whisper, "He likes to fight."[21] Russert got it right. But the big question isn't whether McCain likes to fight: it's who, when, and how.

FOUR

War, What Is It Good For?

If you get involved in a major ground war in the Saudi desert,
I think support will erode significantly. Nor should it be
supported. We cannot even contemplate, in my view, trading
American blood for Iraqi blood.

John McCain, *New York Times*, August 19, 1990

But there is nothing nuanced about his position on the Iraq
war. In speeches on and off the Senate floor and in countless
television interviews, McCain has argued that it was right to
remove Saddam Hussein and that the United States and its
allies must remain in Iraq until conditions are created for a
stable, secure Iraqi government.

David Broder, *Washington Post*, November 20, 2005

ON THE ISSUE OF FOREIGN POLICY interventions,
and specifically on troop deployment on the ground
in Iraq, McCain has made a complete 180-degree turn
from his stated beliefs during his traditional "noninterventionist" conservative phase of the 1980s and early to
mid-1990s. During that time, he was still under the sway
of Goldwater Republicanism and perhaps his own mem-
ories of Vietnam—not exactly a triumphant exercise of
American power.

Today, of course, McCain promotes himself as a war hero and foreign policy expert—as if one led inevitably to the other. More specifically—and dangerously—he comports himself as an expert on what we should do in Iraq. He supported the Iraq war from the beginning while carping about its execution. He put all his chips on the 2007 surge, and though the United States is nowhere near the high-minded goals it announced in the run-up to the invasion, McCain's supporters would have us believe that he's Churchill reborn. Not everyone, however, is buying it. Paul Rieckhoff, founder of the Iraq and Afghanistan Veterans of America (IAVA) and author of a bestselling book about his experience as a platoon leader in Iraq, described McCain's Iraq policy to me as follows: "It's half-assed, it's not going to work, he's being inconsistent in supporting it, and yet still seems to support it for political reasons."

History may show that McCain was never right about the invasion or the "escalation"—the straight-talk translation of the more emotive "surge." It may show instead that what was needed from the outset was a greater commitment of ground forces, or that we should have stayed out completely. Historians are unlikely to conclude that half measures and torture, in addition to an initially unjustified intervention, was ever brilliant foreign policy. But many observers agree that McCain's current aggressive stance on international issues doesn't square with the cautious isolationism that defined McCain's own positions from the Reagan years through almost the entire Clinton era. At that time, McCain seemed to understand George

Washington's old maxim about being wary of "foreign entanglements."[1] How is it, exactly, that McCain came to support "rogue-state rollback" as a campaign platform in 2000?[2]

LEBANON

In the first decade and a half of his public life, McCain was almost always opposed to deployment. As you read the following, remember, this isn't Hillary Clinton, Barack Obama, or Ron Paul talking about Iraq. This is John McCain talking about the deployment of U.S. Marines to Beirut in 1983.

> I have listened carefully to the explanations offered for our involvement . . . I do not find them convincing. The fundamental question is, "What is the United States' interest . . . ?" It is said we are there to keep the peace. I ask, what peace? It is said we are there to aid the government. I ask, what government? It is said we are there to stabilize the region. I ask, how can the U.S. presence stabilize the region? . . .
>
> The longer we stay . . . the harder it will be for us to leave. We will be trapped . . . What can we expect if we withdraw . . . ? The same as will happen if we stay. I acknowledge that the level of fighting will increase if we leave. I regretfully acknowledge that many innocent civilians will be hurt. But I firmly believe this will happen in any event.
>
> What about our allies and worldwide prestige? We should consult with our allies and withdraw with them in concert if possible, unilaterally if necessary. I also recognize that our

prestige may suffer in the short term, but I am more concerned with our long-term national interests. I believe the
circumstances of our original involvement have changed,
and I know four American families who share this view.

I am not calling for an immediate withdrawal of our
forces. What I desire is as rapid a withdrawal as possible.[3]

He was right, by the way, and he voted against President
Reagan's resolution to deploy Marines in Lebanon. Tragic-
ally, that didn't help the two hundred twenty Marines and
twenty-one other service members who were killed in the
embassy bombing a month later.

SOMALIA

Next up was Somalia. McCain once again argued that we
had no business there. After the invasion of Iraq, Tim
Russert asked him about his criteria for deploying troops
abroad.

Russert: Let me show you the kinds of things that are often said
when soldiers are overseas, like this: "There's no reason for
the United States to remain. The American people want them
home. I believe the majority of Congress wants them home.
Our continued military presence allows another situation to
rise, which could then lead to the wounding, killing or capture
of American fighting men and women. We should do all in our
power to avoid that. What should be the criteria is our immediate, orderly withdrawal? And if we do not do that and other
Americans die then I say that the responsibilities for that lie

with the Congress who did not exercise their authority under the Constitution. For us to get into nation-building, law and order, etcetera, I think, is a tragic and terrible mistake." You hear those kinds of words, right?

McCain: Sure I do. Americans are frustrated and saddened by the enormous sacrifice we've made and the gross mismanagement of the war. Now, my response to that statement is, and what happens after we leave? Listen to all of the experts who will tell you that we can have a situation in the region which will, in, in the long run, entail far greater casualties, far greater dislocation, far greater threats to our national security than trying to give this an opportunity to succeed. That's what the—my response to that heartfelt statement is.

Russert: Well, those are your words from 1993 about Somalia . . .

McCain: Well, if you compare—want to compare Somalia to what's at stake in Iraq, please feel free to do so. I don't see any comparison except that there was chaos in the streets of Mogadishu, and this now [Iraq] is [*sic*] got to do with vital national security interests.[4]

McCain implied that Russert was comparing apples to oranges. But many credible sources have argued that Somalia was our first engagement with Al Qaeda, which was aiding and training the Somalis.[5] If anything, there was more reason to be in Somalia than in Iraq. But candidate McCain, who was dead wrong on weapons of mass destruction in Iraq, would have us believe now that the anti-interventionism he favored in Somalia and Lebanon is tantamount to surrender.

HAITI

The isolationism continued with Haiti in 1994. McCain was eager to pack up and go home. Seeing no vital interest at stake in civil unrest off our shores, he argued on the Senate floor in October of that year for withdrawal.

> In my view that does not mean as soon as order is restored to Haiti. It does not mean as soon as democracy is flourishing in Haiti. It does not mean as soon as we have established a viable nation in Haiti. As soon as possible means as soon as we can get out of Haiti without losing any American lives.[6]

Years later, candidate McCain would argue the exact opposite: that we must establish order, stability, and a viable nation before we withdraw from Iraq.

BOSNIA AND KOSOVO

Yet, in May 1995 McCain took the same attitude toward U.S. involvement in Bosnia that he had expressed regarding Beirut, Haiti, and Somalia. In his usual brash manner, McCain declared quite matter of factly that Bosnia did not affect America's "vital national interests."[7] Although not a single U.S. soldier was lost in our effort there, McCain glumly warned that those efforts were "doomed to failure from the beginning, when we believed that we could keep peace in a place where there was no peace."[8] On this issue, McCain was quoted disapprovingly by Republican Representative Vin Weber of Minnesota in the *National Review*.

Why are these Republicans balking at taking action in Bosnia? Senator McCain, a leader of the Republican doves, says it is a question of our capabilities. "There is an understandable guilt we all feel about having done nothing to stop the Holocaust . . . But the question is: What is viable? We cannot confuse a desire to do good with viable military options."[9]

A leader of the Republican doves! How quaint. It took a year for McCain, after originally opposing the intervention of U.S. ground troops in Bosnia to prevent genocide, to come around and support intervention. Once he did change his mind, he became a cosponsor of the resolution *supporting* the inclusion of ground troops.[10]

It was sometime after Bosnia that McCain transformed from Goldwater isolationist to General Buck Turgidson from *Doctor Strangelove*. Did McCain simply need a base in the GOP for his presidential run? Since that base didn't include religious or economic conservatives, perhaps he chose to fly like a hawk.

Some veterans, however, are unimpressed by the transformation. Major Paul Hackett, who ran for an Ohio congressional seat after returning from Iraq, told me with his characteristic bluntness that McCain's foreign policy "shows the same dishonesty as his actions regarding Jerry Falwell and Pat Robertson. Most of this country knows they're extremists, and McCain in the past lambasted these clowns. But now he's sucking up to them."[11]

The *Boston Globe* reported the foreign policy metamorphosis in 1999:

[McCain] did not originally call for military intervention in
Kosovo. But when he examined the initial air strikes against
Yugoslavia, he concluded there was no way NATO could oust
Serbian forces in Kosovo without a credible threat of ground
troops. McCain stated that he fully supported the NATO
effort in Kosovo, and seemed to benefit politically from his
newfound hawkishness. . . .[12]

McCain, described by columnist William Safire at the
time as "the de facto president of the United States," became one of the nation's strongest voices in favor of the
Kosovo war, and saw his poll numbers rise quickly into
double digits in the months before the New Hampshire
primary. At the same time, Bush, the campaign's frontrunner—who expressed unease at American intervention and "nation-building"—appeared to dither on the
subject.[13]

Changing one's mind in response to fresh information
is no vice, but in the case of Bosnia and Kosovo, McCain's
reversal looks suspiciously like a flip-flop. His changing
positions only further obfuscate whatever core convictions
he may, or may not, possess in the foreign policy arena.

IRAQ—ROUND ONE

McCain's foreign policy journey can also be traced through
his evolving attitude toward Saddam Hussein and Iraq.
In the 1980s Reagan Republicans had an ally in Saddam
Hussein. That was when arming Iraq was the smart move
to counter the revolution in Iran. (It was also when arming

Osama bin Laden and others in Afghanistan was a shrewd way to contain Soviet expansion.)

Then came Iraq's invasion of Kuwait. That threatened U.S. oil interests, so policy was adjusted accordingly. At first Senator McCain called for a measured response. "I think that we have to make use of the advantages we have, and that is through the air."[64] But as for ground troops, he wasn't biting. No way, no how. In 1990 he said, "We cannot even contemplate, in my view, trading American blood for Iraqi blood."[14]

President Bush (the elder) and others in Congress thought differently. A congressional resolution authorized President Bush to put ground troops in Iraq. At that point, McCain supported the resolution. He also supported the administration's decision not to march into Baghdad when the Gulf War was in its final days.

Yet as the 1990s came to a close, the situation in Iraq had become intolerable to McCain. In 1998 he joined a group of neoconservatives calling for the removal of Saddam Hussein. "Our ability to ensure that Saddam Hussein is not producing weapons of mass destruction . . . has substantially diminished," they wrote to President Clinton. "The only acceptable strategy is one that eliminates the possibility that Iraq will be able to use or threaten to use weapons of mass destruction." In their view, there was no time to secure UN authorization for a military strike, as is required by the international laws the United States helped to implement in the aftermath of World War II. Now these very laws were a danger to the United States. "American policy," the letter declared, "cannot continue to be crippled by a misguided insistence on unanimity in the UN Security Council." Failure to act as these wise councillors recommended would "put our interests and our future at risk." The signatories included Paul Wolfowitz, Donald Rumsfeld, John Bolton, Richard Perle, Elliot Abrams, William Kristol, and Zalmay Khalilzad.[15]

What should voters make of the company McCain was keeping? At the very least, this group bears significant responsibility for the decimation of Iraqi society as well as the American blood spilled and treasure spent to invade and occupy that country. Its concerns about Saddam's weapons of mass destruction, or WMDs, were misplaced—so much so that the very policies they so forcefully recommended "put our interests and our future at risk."

Candidate McCain would have us believe that his experience and leadership will help us in Iraq. But if it weren't for McCain and his colleagues, we likely never would have gone there.

FIVE

Staying the Course

Despite the fact that no weapons of mass destruction were found in Iraq, McCain said he was convinced that Saddam Hussein, the deposed Iraqi dictator, eventually would have tried to acquire those weapons and use them against the United States. "Bush," McCain said, "has sent a message to despots everywhere that 'their day is done.'"

St. Paul Pioneer Press, September 4, 2004

LACKING A BASE AMONG SOCIAL, Christian, and economic conservatives as he geared up for the 2000 presidential bid, McCain needed an effective way to reach Republican voters. How about foreign policy?

After spending time with pseudo-wonks who double as purveyors of military wisdom, he began pushing out foreign policy manifestos calling for "rogue-state rollback."[1] These efforts made McCain the candidate of choice in the 2000 campaign for the leading neoconservatives, from William Safire to William Kristol. McCain also gained the support of Charles Krauthammer, Norman Podhoretz, and others who figured he would be more likely than George

W. Bush to deliver what they sought in the Middle East: misery.

But that support didn't protect McCain from Karl Rove's attack machine in South Carolina. After 9/11, Bush became the neocons' man, and McCain became Bush's loyal soldier. He proudly carried the democracy-through-war banner for Bush, Rumsfeld, Cheney, and Wolfowitz.

The neocons brushed aside McCain's flip-flopping on foreign policy issues and welcomed the war hero into their fold. McCain's tough-guy image fit perfectly with Leo Strauss's project to create myths (or "noble lies") to maintain a cohesive society.[2] So McCain pitched in to sell the war through the media, which ate up his Sunday morning reassurances that the war was necessary and would shortly be over.

To bolster his position, McCain threw his arm around Senator Joe Lieberman. Lieberman agreed to serve as co-chair of the Committee on the Liberation of Iraq (CLI), an offshoot of the infamous Project for a New American Century. This group of elite McCainiacs—who have gotten everything about Iraq wrong—was comprised largely of signatories to a September 2001 public letter to President Bush calling for the United States to go after Hamas, Hezbollah, Syria, Iraq, Iran, and North Korea.

One character at the center of this project, Randy Scheunemann, is largely credited with bringing McCain into the neoconservative fold and creating the rogue-state rollback strategy. Beginning in 2000, when Scheunemann became a key advisor, McCain sought to distinguish himself from other Republican presidential candidates and House isolationists. McCain began reading the Murdoch-owned *Weekly Standard* and conferring with its editors, especially Bill Kristol.[3]

Scheunemann joined Richard Perle and Paul Wolfowitz on another bright idea: giving approximately $350,000 per month in taxpayer money to Iraqi National Congress kingpin Ahmad Chalabi. As we now know, Chalabi lied to the United States about Saddam Hussein's capabilities and purportedly passed on classified U.S. intelligence to his friends in Iran. The thought that Scheunemann—also a former aide to Trent Lott and Donald Rumsfeld—might one day become a national security advisor in a McCain administration is sobering.

TODAY I STARTED A WAR

In March 2003, the efforts of McCain and his new friends came to fruition; they got their war. A war that Paul Rieckhoff, a self-described "political Independent," told me was "poorly conceived, badly communicated, and horribly executed."[4] A war that former covert operative, counterterrorism advisor, and commentator Larry Johnson told me led to a "fundamental change in attitude among the military, in terms of who they trust and support politically." The military, Johnson said, "look at what McCain and company have done over there and realize it's a complete shit sandwich."[5]

Since the war in Iraq began, McCain hasn't stopped sup-

porting it, but he has waffled repeatedly on important issues related to the war. Many people see plenty of inconsis-
tency, contradiction, and hypocrisy, especially when there's
an American body count involved. Not so McCain's ador-
ing fans in the national media. Even when they know the
straight-talker is lying, they just can't bring themselves to say
so. Take this piece from *Time* magazine scribe Joe Klein:

> McCain, whether you agree with him or not, has been
> entirely consistent about the war . . . I admire McCain's
> honorable willingness to take this unpopular position into
> the 2008 election . . . which makes it even more disappoint-
> ing when the Senator slides into political calculation, as he
> does when he challenges those who oppose the escalation to
> cut off funding for the war.[6]

At least Klein was willing to call out McCain for his "political calculation" regarding Iraq policy. But Greg Sargent
of *Talking Points Memo* points out the obvious: "Let me be
civil about this," begins Sargent, "McCain has *not* been 'entirely consistent' about the war. In fact, he's been quite
inconsistent in two key areas: first, in the amount of additional troops he's said are required in Iraq; and second, in
his assessments of how the war's been going over the past
couple years."[7]

When Bush proposed sending an additional 21,500
troops to Iraq, McCain said he preferred to send even
more—but only after he was on record as saying that a
lower number would suffice. Again, Sargent:

You can't volunteer a number that you say you think will work and then turn around and say that you're worried that a *larger* number might *not* work and that you actually wanted to send *more* than that larger number. That's not consistent at all.

Sargent also wondered about the way McCain has dealt with officers trying to execute this misbegotten war.

The other day, for instance, McCain "grilled" General George Casey at a Senate hearing, blasting Casey by saying that over the past two and a half years, "things have gotten markedly and progressively worse" in Iraq. But even a cursory bit of research shows that this criticism from McCain was completely inconsistent with his own past statements. During the same period that McCain said he saw things get "markedly and progressively worse," McCain himself repeatedly offered optimistic assessments and even said several times that things were *improving* in Iraq.[8]

These inconvenient truths have not made it into the vast majority of reporting on the "straight talker." According to one report by *U.S. News & World Report*'s Gloria Borger, "No one would accuse McCain of equivocating on anything."[9] Really? I would. And the facts would back me up.

The kid-glove treatment of McCain is all too common in the media, as David Brock and Paul Waldman point out in their recent book, *Free Ride: John McCain and the Media*. It explains why McCain is the only sitting senator to host

Saturday Night Live and why Don Imus endorses him.[10] And it's probably why he polls well across many segments of the electorate: people believe that the war hero knows what he's talking about and isn't a political calculator.

For whatever reason, the media haven't underscored other examples of McCain's flip-flopping on Iraq. In January 2008, McCain claimed on MSNBC that he *knew* the war in Iraq was "probably going to be long and hard and tough," and that he was "sorry" for those who voted for the war believing it would be "some kind of an easy task." Why on earth would they think that? "Maybe they didn't know what they were voting for," McCain offered.[11]

Let's go to the videotape. Senator McCain on CNN, September 24, 2002: "Because I know that as successful as I believe we will be, and I believe that the success will be fairly easy, we will still lose some American young men or women." And here's McCain on MSNBC in January 2003: "But the point is that . . . we will win this conflict. We will win it easily."[12]

Political observer Glenn Greenwald summarizes McCain's position on Iraq this way: "1) in order to win in Iraq, we need to expand our military by 100,000 more troops; 2) we don't have anywhere near 100,000 troops to send to Iraq, and nobody suggests that we do; 3) a draft is absolutely unnecessary."[13] Even on its own preferred terms, McCain's plan doesn't add up.

Here's how his fantasy played out with Chris Matthews on *Hardball*, as quoted by Greenwald:

Matthews: You've called, just in the last couple of days, for 100,000 more troops on top of the 140,000 we have as a complement there. When I read that on the clips this morning, I went to General Barry McCaffrey, whom you know so well. He says we simply don't have the capability to sustain another 100,000 troops in Iraq. You disagree?

McCain: I said we need 100,000 more—

Matthews: Right.

McCain: —members of the Marines and the army. We need additional troops there, but I think we need to expand the army and the Marine Corps by 100,000 people.[14]

But as Donald Rumsfeld said, we went to war with the army we had.

Other high-profile observers and decision-makers have faulted McCain's support of President Bush's surge. Republican Chuck Hagel suggested that because McCain knows the surge strategy will ultimately fail, his support for the escalation is "intellectually dishonest."[15] Zbigniew Brzezinski, a foreign policy elder statesmen respected on both sides of the aisle, called McCain's position "a gimmick, because it satisfies . . . the hardliners."[16] Combine this dishonesty with McCain's absences during Iraq war votes, and you can't help but agree with Sargent, Hagel, Brzezinski, and others that McCain has traded principle for politics at the cost of many young soldiers who have returned seriously wounded or in body bags.

For those of you keeping score at home, let's get the

sequence right. In 1990 McCain said he couldn't "contemplate . . . trading American blood for Iraqi blood."[17] Less than a decade later, McCain assured the American people that the invasion of Iraq was necessary. In 2002, as a supporter of a ground invasion of Iraq, he said, "We're not going to get into house-to-house fighting . . . We may have to take out buildings, but we're not going to have a bloodletting of trading American bodies for Iraqi bodies."[18] He also told us the invasion of Iraq would be easy. Then he said people who thought it would be easy weren't paying attention. Then he told us we needed a hundred thousand more troops.

But for quite a while before that, he told us that mostly we needed to stay the course.

- On *ABC News,* October 24, 2004, McCain said, "Is Afghanistan perfect, no, we've got opium, we've got warlords, but by God, it's a heck of a lot better off than it was. And we can to do the same thing in Iraq, we've got to stay the course."[19]

- *CBS Early Show,* June 29, 2005: "We need some successes. But, also, I am heartened by the fact that 58 percent of the American people, according to a . . . *Washington Post* poll, yesterday, say that we've got to stay the course."[20]

- *The Hill,* December 8, 2005: "I think the situation on the ground is going to improve. Overall, I think a year from now, we will have made a fair amount of progress if we stay the course."[21]

But in October 2006, during a speech in West Virginia, McCain executed a 180-degree turn. According to the *Charleston Gazette,* "McCain acknowledged that 'many, many mistakes' had been made in Iraq" and that he "was not an advocate for a 'stay the course' policy in Iraq."[22]

REDEPLOYMENT

McCain has attacked Democrats for supporting "redeployment" in Iraq. His criticism, it seems, is that redeployment is a code word for a tactical withdrawal to secure Iraq's borders. That move would leave the Iraqis to fight it out among themselves, and that would be tantamount to surrender.

Initially, however, McCain called for something that sounded suspiciously like redeployment in an interview with the *Politico*: "If this strategy doesn't succeed, we will have to devise another strategy," McCain said. "But I have to hasten to add there are no good options." One of those options, McCain said, "is to withdraw to the borders (of Iraq) to try to keep other countries from interfering. Maintaining our bases in Kuwait and other places. There are a lot of scenarios." But he also said the current troop surge strategy "has to be given time."[23] "Withdrawing to the borders of Iraq"? Did McCain mean redeployment?

Now consider his answer, less than a week after the *Politico* interview, to a query by CNN's Anderson Cooper. Cooper wanted to know whether success would be a prerequisite for redeploying troops. McCain replied, "That's my view."[24] Apparently redeployment was no longer an option.

Once McCain decided that redeployment was unacceptable, all bets were off. If you disagreed, you were willing to see the United States defeated by Al Qaeda. That much was clear from McCain's response to Hillary Clinton when she offered a scenario similar to the one McCain advanced in the *Politico*:

> Senator Clinton wants to raise the white flag and surrender in Iraq . . . We will not surrender, my friends. The strategy is succeeding. We're not going to have for the first time a major candidate in history declare surrender. That's not gonna happen on my watch. It's not going to happen. And that's going to be a big issue in this debate. We have succeeded and we can win. We're not going to let Senator Clinton snatch defeat from the jaws of victory. That's not going to happen. We will never wave the white flag to Al Qaida and surrender, my friends.[25]

His determination sounds impressive. But when will the United States be able to declare victory and leave Iraq? McCain seems unsure. In April 2007, many years into the occupation, he executed a perfect forty-seven-second flip-flop on *This Week with George Stephanopoulos*:

McCain: Took us a long time to get in the situation we're in, and to say that—and somehow assume that in a few months, that things are going to get all better I think is not realistic.

Stephanopoulos: You say it's all in. How long are you going to give it to work?

McCain: I think in the case of the Iraqi government cooperating and doing what's necessary, we can know fairly well in a few months.[26]

A TRUST ISSUE

Once the occupation began and the U.S. policy resembled trading American bodies for Iraqi bodies, McCain's descriptions of the conflict became untrustworthy. When an April 2007 CBS poll asked if McCain accurately conveyed what was going on in Iraq, 39 percent of respondents said he made things seem "better than they really are." Only 29 percent thought he gave them an accurate impression.[27] McCain has been called out several times on those discrepancies, especially as they concern the safety level in Baghdad since the surge. For example, he was forced to disavow his assertion that General Petraeus rides "almost every day in an unarmored Humvee."[28]

But it was his depiction of his journey through a Baghdad marketplace in March 2007 that raised the most ire. On Bill Bennett's radio show, he said he had just returned from a neighborhood in Baghdad "where you and I could walk today."[29] During an April 1, 2007, press conference, he said that "things are better" in Baghdad, despite all evidence to the contrary.[30] Local merchants contradicted McCain's account, saying that life in Baghdad had become much more dangerous.[31] CNN's Michael Ware, reporting from the streets of Baghdad, said that military sources greeted McCain's comments yesterday with "laughter down the line."[32] The derision probably stemmed from McCain's own security needs during his Baghdad stroll: a bullet-proof vest, an escort of one hundred soldiers, three Black Hawk helicopters, and two Apache gunships.

Larry Johnson noted an even more significant cause for outrage at McCain's ploy: soldiers had to leave their normal routines to sweep the market for bombs, snipers had to be put in place, and commanders had to draw up a plan for the publicity stunt. As Johnson put it, "McCain placed soldiers' lives at risk for a photo-op." With a rising level of anger in his voice, Johnson continued: "If you're willing to do that, and like him you *know better*, then your ambition has made you a risk to our men and women in uniform."[33]

A WAR-LIKE TEMPER

How has McCain's temperament held up during this time? Hoisting himself on his own petard of straight talk has made McCain grumpy, so much so that *Rolling Stone* columnist Matt Taibbi described McCain as an "aneurysm-in-waiting."[34]

Various Democrats and media figures have raised his ire by challenging him on his foreign policy inconsistencies. McCain attacked author and *Huffington Post* proprietor Arianna Huffington at the Davos Economic Forum in Switzerland when she dared to ask follow-up questions about his position on the surge in Iraq. After offering her detailed description of the incident, Huffington noted, "Suddenly, with McCain out of the room, the debate in the room shifted away from Iraq and onto McCain's temper, with the consensus being summed up by Anatol Kaletsky of the *London Times*: 'It appears that his short fuse will become a problem for him during the campaign.'"[35]

McCain's temper sometimes shows itself as passive aggression, as when he told fellow veteran Representative John Murtha (D-PA) "to lighten up and get a life." Murtha had objected to McCain's "joke" on the *Daily Show* that he had a present—an IED, or improvised explosive device—for television host Jon Stewart.[36] But one can hardly blame Murtha for being angered by the tasteless joke and McCain's boorish defense of it.

McCain has also taken to chastising Democrats who fail to support every war-related decision made by the Bush administration and its supporters. On *Meet the Press* in January 2007, McCain spoke about the Democrats' non-binding resolution denouncing the surge plan.

> [T]his resolution is basically a vote of no confidence in the men and women we are sending over there. We're saying, "We're sending you—we're not going to stop you from going there, but we don't believe you can succeed and we're not willing to support that." I don't think the troops would find that an expression of support. And to accuse the president of the United States of, quote, "rushing troops over there" is beneath, frankly, the behavior level that I think is appropriate for members of Congress.[37]

No examination of McCain's partisan behavior regarding the war in Iraq would be complete without some reference to McCain's speech disparaging House Democrats for voting to set a timeline for withdrawal for U.S. troops from Iraq: "Democratic leaders smiled and cheered as the last votes were counted," said McCain. "What were they celebrating? Defeat? Surrender? In Iraq, only our enemies were cheering."[38]

This was a bridge too far for another Vietnam veteran, Senator Jim Webb of Virginia:

> I'm disappointed in John McCain. I've known him for many years. The day before we begin the debate on the Iraq bills, he pulled me aside on the Senate floor and said, 'Jim, we do not want the situation we had in the Vietnam War. We do not want one side impugning the patriotism of the other side,' and [yet] John McCain has been doing this consistently since that time. I don't believe that it is in anybody's interest for members of the Senate to be impugning the other side's patriotism, or by the way, to be hiding behind the troops as political justification for what we're doing.[39]

As in the case of the Baghdad market stroll, there was another massive irony in McCain's criticism of House Democrats. "A defeat for the United States is a cause for mourning, not celebrating," said McCain. "And determining how the United States can avert such a disaster should encourage the most sober, public-spirited reasoning among our elected leaders, not the giddy anticipation of the next election." But as Greg Sargent noted, "McCain is running for president, and this speech was being described by his own aides as critical to reinvigorating his campaign."[40]

AFTER IRAQ, THE WORLD

If you like what McCain has done with Iraq, you'll love what he seems to have planned for Iran, North Korea, and the rest of the world. Iraq is not the only place where John McCain would have our overstretched, underfunded military continue to fight.

When asked on what issue he most strenuously disagreed with candidate John Kerry during the 2004 presidential campaign, McCain identified North Korea. In McCain's view, the United States shouldn't hold talks with North Korea. In fact, when it comes to dealing with this isolated country and its seemingly irrational dictator, it appears McCain's first thought is to attack . . . *Democrats*. Specifically, when North Korea conducted a nuclear test in October 2006, McCain blamed former President Clinton. Senator Hillary Clinton's office quickly responded: "A missile shield alone cannot protect us from the Bush-Cheney administration's incompetence in their approach to Iraq, Iran, and North Korea, and it is unfortunate that Republicans such as John McCain continue to blindly defend their failed policies for partisan gain rather than exercise true leadership."[41] McCain's reaction? To decry finger-pointing.

McCain would also have the United States refuse to deal with Iran, a country significantly strengthened by the war in Iraq. McCain famously sang his updated version of an old Beach Boys favorite when he was asked at Murrells Inlet VFW Hall in South Carolina when he thought the U.S. military "might send an air mail message to Tehran."[42] The song has the words "bomb" and "Iran" in it. Six months later, he promised to bomb Iran if we suspect it is getting nuclear weapons.[43]

Most Americans oppose this lunacy. According to numerous polls, including one conducted by *Fox News* in June 2006, 59 percent of Americans favor talking with Iran—even if it continues on the path to becoming a nuclear state. But McCain has taken to the Bush plan, which is to threaten attacks against Iran. And in October 2006, the Program on International Policy Attitudes (PIPA) asked whether the United States should hold talks with Iran and North Korea without preconditions. Of the 55 percent that responded affirmatively, 56 percent described themselves as political independents—the moderates McCain claims to represent. According to the PIPA poll, only 28 percent of respondents thought the United States should engage in the Bush-McCain plan to help dissidents overthrow the Iranian government.[44]

On foreign policy, the thinking of most Americans and that of John McCain diverge—widely. With McCain as commander in chief, will more Americans die in a war that never should have been fought? What will the intemperate war hero do when taunted by Iranian president Mahmoud Ahmadinejad? Will he have the cool to keep us safe, or will he throw caution to the wind, equate diplomacy with weakness, and pull the trigger? Many of us would rather not find out.

SIX

Reform? We Don't Need No Stinkin' Reform

Have you heard of lobbyists? They do very bad things that have destroyed our great nation, according to John McCain, which is why everybody with any involvement in his doomed campaign is required to be a practicing lobbyist. The current "revolving door" batch of lobbyists who run his entire life include lobbyists for Verizon, SBC, AT&T, Alcoa, J.P. Morgan, U.S. Airways, Land O' Lakes, General Motors, United Technologies, UST Public Affairs, eBay, Goldman Sachs Group, Cablevision, Tenneco, Novartis Pharmaceuticals, Dell, Fannie Mae, Southwest Airlines, Toyota and the Pharmaceutical Research and Manufacturers of America.

Wonkette, February 22, 2008

"THE VOICES OF AVERAGE AMERICANS have been drowned out by the deafening racket of campaign cash."[1] This is the populist appeal John McCain is using in his attempt to win the allegiance of average Americans. In reality, he has flip-flopped multiple times on all manner of reform while continually doing the bidding of big business.

When it comes to money and politics, McCain's history

doesn't live up to his "reformer" or "straight talker" standards. The better question, it seems, is whether or not he meets the normal standard of Congressional behavior.

THE KEATING SAGA

McCain didn't begin his political life as a campaign finance reformer. Some of his worst behavior occurred when he was launching his political career. Between 1982 and 1987, McCain accepted $112,000 in campaign contributions from Charles H. Keating, the CEO of American Continental Corporation, as well as his family members and employees.[2] In 1986 McCain's wife Cindy and father-in-law Jim Hensley invested about $359,000 in a Keating shopping center in Phoenix.[3] McCain, his family, and on occasion their babysitter made "at least nine trips" aboard an American Continental jet, at Keating's expense.[4] One frequent destination was the Bahamas, where McCain could ponder the interests of his many working- and middle-class constituents in comfort. According to House rules, McCain was required to disclose these flights, but he neglected to do so until the scandal went public in 1989.

When the investigation of Keating began in 1987—he was suspected of defrauding Lincoln Savings & Loan investors to the tune of $285 million—McCain and four other senators met with federal regulators. One wonders what was said. Despite a plethora of evidence at their disposal, the regulators didn't seize Keating's business for two more years. Or maybe it didn't matter what was said; maybe what really mattered was that Keating got five U.S. Senators to show up at the meeting.

The regulators eventually confiscated Lincoln, and Keating was convicted of 73 counts of wire and bankruptcy fraud. His state conviction was overturned on a technicality, but he served four years on the federal conviction. Bankruptcy protection shielded him from having to pay back all the people whose lives he destroyed; 17,000 Lincoln investors lost $190 million. The taxpayers weren't so lucky. We got to pick up the bill, which came to $2.6 billion.

McCain was "rebuked" by the Senate Select Committee on Ethics in 1991—which he considered to be a "full exoneration."[5] This didn't sit well with his fellow Arizona senator, Democrat Dennis DeConcini, who declared that McCain had received special treatment from the Senate Ethics Committee's counsel, Robert Bennett, the high-powered lawyer who also turned up to defend McCain in February 2008 against charges that he handed out favors to the clients of lobbyist Vicki Iseman.

In the Keating case, Bennett found McCain and Senator John Glenn of Ohio to be less culpable than their colleagues. But DeConcini wasn't pleased with some of Bennett's methods. According to a *New York Times* story in 1990:

> Mr. DeConcini asked why Mr. Bennett had not pressed Mr. McCain about his family's trips to Mr. Keating's vacation home in the Bahamas or about his wife's investments with Mr. Keating.
>
> He also accused Mr. Bennett of having discussions with

Mr. McCain before taking his sworn deposition. "What Mr. Bennett did for Senator McCain is permit him to have an interview with his lawyer before they took his deposition," Mr. DeConcini said. "So it was pretty cozy, wasn't it?"[6]

In the aftermath of the Keating scandal, McCain managed to shed his tattered ethics and don the mantle of a fierce campaign-finance crusader. The new McCain developed a reputation for standing up to greedy corporations and venal politicians. But McCain 2.0 was not—and is not—the Real McCain.

HELLO, CAMPAIGN FINANCE REFORM

A key part of McCain's metamorphosis was his work with Senator Russ Feingold (D-WI). That work focused on setting campaign spending limits, eliminating soft money given to the political parties in unregulated amounts by corporations and unions, allotting free television time to lower the cost of running political campaigns, and setting restrictions on what "independent" groups (like the Swift Boat Veterans for Truth) can do to influence an election. Some of these measures, most notably the ban on soft money, were ultimately passed as part of the Bipartisan Campaign Finance Reform Act in 2002.[7]

But there were many signs along the way that hinted that McCain's conversion was a matter of political opportunism, not deep principle. In January 1995, for example, McCain voted to kill an amendment proposed by John

Kerry to prohibit candidates from using campaign contributions for personal needs, including paying themselves a salary.[8] He also voted against another Kerry amendment to continue the public financing of elections.[9] Nor was he shy in the fundraising department. By February 2000, nine months shy of the 2000 election, McCain had raised $121,000 from lobbyists alone.[10]

Between his two presidential campaigns, an all-too-familiar side of McCain's political personality emerged. Anyone who didn't see campaign finance reform exactly his way was subject to threat, intimidation, or mockery. In March 2008, conservative pundit George Will criticized McCain's tendency to walk one way, talk another, and then berate, threaten, or attack those who don't follow his lead. Here's how Will told the story.

> In 2001, McCain, a situational ethicist regarding "big money" in politics, founded the Reform Institute to lobby for his agenda of campaign restrictions. It accepted large contributions, some of six figures, from corporations with business before the Commerce Committee (e.g., Echosphere, DISH Network, Cablevision Systems Corporation, a charity funded by the head of Univision) . . . Although his campaign is run by lobbyists; and although his dealings with lobbyists have generated what he, when judging the behavior of others, calls corrupt appearances; and although he has profited from his manipulation of the taxpayer-funding system that is celebrated by reformers—still, he probably is innocent of insincerity. Such is his towering

moral vanity, he seems sincerely to consider it theoretically impossible for him to commit the offenses of appearances that he incessantly ascribes to others.[11]

That same moral vanity has led McCain to pick fights with fellow reformers as well. Two sources (neither at Common Cause) who spoke on condition of anonymity told me about McCain's attempts to remove former president of Common Cause, Chellie Pingree, from her job. Common Cause, a non-partisan group devoted to open government, was in some ways the field operative for McCain-Feingold in the Senate. But soon, according to my sources, Pingree saw that this regulatory scheme was too full of loopholes; in particular, she realized that it would lead to too much confusion about what various sorts of organizations could or could not do.

Like many others at that time, Pingree concluded that straightforward public financing was the answer. This wasn't what McCain wanted to hear. In an effort to remove Pingree, McCain's operatives made phone calls to Common Cause board members, funders, and anyone else they thought they could persuade or intimidate. McCain's efforts failed, but they showed that he was willing to attack an ally the moment her judgment veered away from his own.

Once McCain decided to run for president again, these differences became moot. He realized he would benefit in the presidential sweepstakes if he treated campaign finance reform as he'd once treated Chellie Pingree—as something to be left behind. The new strategy was on clear display as McCain 3.0 marched toward the White House. A *Washington Post* article offers a snapshot from early 2008:

> [W]hen McCain huddled with his closest advisers at his rustic Arizona cabin last weekend to map out his presidential campaign, virtually everyone was part of the Washington lobbying culture he has long decried. His campaign manager, Rick Davis, co-founded a lobbying firm whose clients have included Verizon and SBC Telecommunications. His chief political adviser, Charles R. Black Jr., is chairman of one of Washington's lobbying powerhouses, BKSH and Associates, which has represented AT&T, Alcoa, JPMorgan and U.S. Airways. Senior advisers Steve Schmidt and Mark McKinnon work for firms that have lobbied for Land O'Lakes, UST Public Affairs, Dell and Fannie Mae.[12]

It ain't pretty, people. Big-time lobbyists have burrowed deeply into the McCain campaign this time around.

GOODBYE, CAMPAIGN FINANCE REFORM

McCain's zigzags on campaign finance have been difficult to track. But just to scratch the surface, let's consider the matter of providing public financing for presidential campaigns. After McCain rejected that approach in 1995, he supported it as part of his rehabilitation project. Yet, when it again became politically inconvenient, McCain's name disappeared from the relevant legislation. In July 2006 Josh Gerstein of the *New York Sun* summed up McCain's most recent course correction.

> On Wednesday, Senator Feingold, a Democrat of Wisconsin, Rep. Martin Meehan, a Democrat of Massachusetts, and Rep. Christopher Shays, a Republican of Connecticut introduced a bill to revive the crumbling system for public financing of presidential campaigns. The bill is largely identical to a measure all four men introduced in 2003, but this time around Mr. McCain is not on board . . . [S]everal people involved in discussions about the legislation said the senator's absence was related to his widely expected bid for the presidency in 2008.[13]

The *New York Times* noticed, too. Its editorial the following month noted that "Senator McCain is a likely candidate for president in 2008, and he is undoubtedly aware that both political parties believe their nominees will have to abandon public financing to stay competitive."[14] Translation: McCain would vacuum up the money as fast as he could.

McCain now shies away from discussing his past as a campaign-finance reformer. In response to a question from ABC's Terry Moran about how much his presidential campaign might cost, McCain shook his head: "I don't want to talk about . . . you know, I'll just talk about anything else you want, but I'm bored with this one."[15]

Sometimes he seems almost mortified by his past association with this issue. In a March 2007 piece in the *New York*

Sun, Bob Bauer comments on McCain's attempts to distance himself from it: "[H]e was the sponsor and leading light of this reform. And yet, he comes off as determined to make as little of his achievement as possible." In an interview, Bauer noted, McCain quickly conceded that the law would be tested in the courts. Only moments before, however, McCain included Antonin Scalia, an ardent opponent of campaign-finance reform, as one of his model Supreme Court justices. "This is a sad day for freedom of speech," Mr. Scalia had written in his dissenting opinion when the Supreme Court upheld the bulk of McCain-Feingold in 2003.[16]

Even during his reforming days, however, McCain energetically raised money from groups with business before the Senate Commerce Committee, which he chaired when his party was in the majority. In January 2000 the *Boston Globe* ran a piece called "McCain Interceded for Donors, Data Show." After noting that McCain had raised nearly $90,000 from broadcast and telecommunications companies shortly before and after he interceded on their behalf with federal regulators in 1998 and 1999, the article goes on to report that McCain was also keeping up with his correspondence.

Aides released about 500 letters that McCain has written as chairman of the Senate Commerce Committee since 1997, and it appeared last night that only 15 involved contributors to his campaigns . . . But in several cases, according to federal campaign finance records that were matched against the letters, the correspondence to the Federal Communications Commission, which McCain's committee oversees, coincided with substantial fund-raising efforts by the companies that stood to benefit from his actions.[17]

In one case, BellSouth officials contributed over $16,000 at a May 1998 fundraiser; four months later, McCain wrote to the FCC, asking that "serious consideration" be given to allowing that company to enter the long-distance market. He also wrote on behalf of AT&T and collected another $25,800 at an October 1998 fundraiser.

Not to be outdone, the satellite television companies got in on the action. McCain also wrote two letters on behalf of Echostar. In between the two mailings, the company's chairman raised about $25,000 for McCain.[18]

Later that year, a CNN.com story tallied up the numbers.

McCain's PAC took in $65,000 from other special interest political action committees through June. About $42,000, or 65%, came from the transportation and telecommunications industries that fall under the jurisdiction of the Commerce Committee...[McCain spokesman Todd] Harris defended the special interest donations. "There's not a single person in Washington who thinks that they can write a check to John McCain and receive any kind of special access," he said.[19]

If Charles Keating was reading this article, he must have been wondering what he had done wrong to get himself caught.

All of this happened way back in 2000. Inquiring minds may want to know if anything has happened along these lines more recently. In a word, yes. In February 2008, McCain again made headlines for his willingness to help donors. Lowell Paxson and his wife donated $10,000 to McCain's PAC within seven months of his sending a letter to the FCC. That letter requested that the FCC make a decision on Paxson's proposed purchase of a Pittsburgh television station. Paxson's colleagues added $20,000 to his donation, and McCain used the company jet, just as he used BellSouth's jet in 2000.

Also at stake was McCain's relationship to Paxson's lobbyist, Vicki Iseman. Much of the media focused on a possible love connection between McCain and Iseman. But the real story was the possible quid pro quo, or perception of same. The *McCain Mutiny*, a conservative anti-McCain blog, neatly summarized that story as follows:

- In 1999, McCain, then chairman of the powerful Senate Commerce Committee, which oversees the FCC, wrote letters to the FCC urging action on a matter that was before the FCC.

- The matter involved Mr. Paxson (and his lobbyist: Vicki Iseman). Mr. Paxson had a financial interest in the outcome of the FCC's decision.

- McCain has said that he didn't meet with Paxson before writing the letters to the FCC (for which McCain was rebuked by the FCC Chairman).

- Paxson says that indeed he did have a meeting with McCain two weeks before the letters were sent.

•   And Paxson attributes the ability to get those meetings to Ms. Iseman.[20]

A coda: FCC chairman William E. Kennard called McCain's decision to write letters on behalf of Paxson "highly unusual."[21]

Finally, there is that little matter of *The People v. Jack Abramoff.* You may remember the tough-talking McCain who investigated Abramoff's illegal dealings while he was the head of the Indian Affairs Committee. In fact, McCain accepted a small donation ($5,000) from Trench Coat Jack before he was busted.[22] And when McCain held a closed-door meeting with nervous GOP lawmakers during the hearings in 2005, he assured them that while his investigation would root out corruption, their ethics would not be one of the matters he would look into.[23] In other words, his investigation was much like O.J.'s search for the real killer.

McCain was missing-in-action for the debate over what kind of lobbying reform was necessary in light of Abramoff's not-so-hostile takeover of the legislative process. And even though McCain offered his own bill, Common Cause director Mike Surrusco noted that it "didn't include any provisions to enforce lobbying regulations."[24]

To understand where McCain now stands on his signature issue, it's helpful to compare his record to that of Russ Feingold, who helped make McCain's reputation as a campaign-finance reformer. Although it has almost cost him his Senate career at least twice now, Feingold has refused to accept PAC money and even rejected Democratic

Party soft money before his and McCain's bill helped outlaw it.

Voters beware: Despite his posturing in the saddle, this old cowboy has lots of scars and saddle bags full of lucre.

Ethics, or the Friends You Keep

Could anyone think of a sadder sight than that of Sen. John McCain, R-Ariz., speaking for President Bush at the Republican National Convention?

Oregonian, September 1, 2004

ALWAYS POLITICALLY EXPEDIENT, John McCain has cast his lot with some shady characters throughout his career. Some have supported him financially, others have been campaign insiders, and still others have been his allies in Congress.

If "follow the money" is one way to understand McCain's career, maybe the best place to start is with those who have filled his campaign coffers. Everyone knows that money is the mother's milk of politics. But for the man who made campaign finance reform his signature issue, the milk soured a few years ago.

FRIENDS IN THE PRIVATE SECTOR

Consider some of McCain's top financial supporters. One
is Houston homebuilder Bob Perry, who the *New York Times*
described as "a prominent donor to Republican committees and candidates" as well as "a major financial backer of
the Swift Boat Veterans for Truth (SBVT), the organization
that assailed the military credentials of 2004 Democratic
presidential nominee John Kerry."[1]

The Swift Boat group was hatched in 2004 to slime the
military record of John Kerry, the Democratic presidential candidate that year. For his service in Vietnam, Kerry
was awarded the Silver Star, the Bronze Star, and three
Purple Hearts. The Swifties—who were funded by major
Republican donors and operatives in Bush's Texas home
base—claimed that Kerry did not deserve his honors and
had greatly exaggerated his heroic actions in battle.

At least one Republican begged to differ. Jim Rassmann,
whose life Kerry saved in Vietnam, registered his disgust
with the SBVT in the *Wall Street Journal.* He wrote that the
Swift Boat television ads were "launched by people without decency," who are "lying," and who "should hang their
heads in shame."[2]

Though John McCain has many times called Kerry a
good friend, he did nothing of substance to help his com-
rade when the Swift Boat ads appeared. He might have used
his political pull, which he earned by campaigning hard
for Bush that year, to persuade the White House to call
off the dogs. But weeks after the ads started and just days

before speaking on Bush's behalf at the 2004 Republican National Convention, McCain blamed the victim. In his view, Kerry had brought on the baseless attacks by talking too much about his Vietnam service.[3] When asked if Bush should insist that the Swifties stop running their ads, McCain said, "Probably, because of the sensitivity of the war issue to me."

Adding insult to injury, McCain has since filled his own war chest with contributions from Swift Boat funders. According to the Federal Election Commission, 8,600 individual contributions of more than $200 each have been made to the Swift Boaters.[4] McCain has gratefully accepted cash to boost his senatorial or presidential aspirations from 262 of these donors. Through February 2008, the contributions of these 262 donors added up to roughly $600,000.[5] (Some of these contributions were made before the Swift Boat organization was created.)

Of the ten men who contributed the most money to the Swift Boat ads, John McCain has accepted money from seven: Bob Perry, Harold Simmons, T. Boone Pickens, Carl Linder Sr., Harlan Crow, Jack E. Caveney, and Albert Huddleston.[6] Bob Perry, for example, contributed $4.5 million to the Swift Boaters and $12,600 to McCain. Likewise, T. Boone Pickens pumped $2 million into smearing Kerry's military service and in 2006 gave $5,000 to McCain's PAC. In November 2007, Pickens surfaced on *Hannity & Colmes* on Fox News to brag about his exploits against Kerry. He said he would give $1 million to anyone who could disprove "even a single charge" flung by the Swifties. "While

I am prepared to show they lied on allegation after allegation," wrote Kerry to Pickens, "you have generously offered to pay one million for just one thing that can be proven false. I am prepared to prove the lie beyond any reasonable doubt."[7] Pickens backed away from his offer.

McCain accepted $2,000 from Sam Fox, who contributed $50,000 to the Swift Boaters. If Fox's name sounds familiar, it's because George W. Bush nominated him for U.S. Ambassador to Belgium in early 2007. When the Senate smelled the Swift Boat stench and signaled its intention to kill his nomination, Bush appointed Fox while Congress was in recess.

Granted, McCain took money from some Swift Boat donors before they contributed to that organization. But long after their ads defamed Kerry, McCain *continued* to take their money. He accepted almost $238,000 in campaign donations from Swift Boaters in 2007 alone. For someone as concerned about his reputation for integrity as McCain, returning donations from Swift Boat bankrollers seems like the least he could do.

It's hard to top the Swift Boaters for the use of sleazy tactics, but McCain has also taken money from the Wyly brothers, Texas businessmen who became friendly with the Bush campaign in 2000. So friendly, in fact, that they spent $2.5 million that year on "independent" ads attacking McCain. In his *Vanity Fair* article, Todd Purdum described McCain's ludicrous flip-flop on these hucksters. The first time around, McCain called them "Wyly coyotes" and implored a Boston audience to tell them "to keep their dirty money in the state of Texas." This time, however, McCain accepted money from the Wylys; in fact, Purdum noted, "The Wylys gave McCain's Straight Talk America political-action committee at least $20,000, and together with other family members and friends they chaired a Dallas fund-raiser for the PAC."[8]

The good news is that McCain actually did return the Wyly brothers' money, but only after they became the subject of a federal investigation.

CAMPAIGN INSIDERS

McCain's campaign staffers haven't all been Boy Scouts, either. Remember McCain's brawl buddy, Congressman Rick Renzi? In September 2006, Citizens for Responsibility and Ethics in Washington (CREW), a nonpartisan watch-dog organization, added Renzi to its list of "the 20 most corrupt members in Congress." In the first three months of 2007 alone, Renzi spent over $100,000 in legal fees in an attempt to fend off the FBI's inquiring minds.[9]

McCain must have been aware of Renzi's character; in fact, he vouched for it when he recorded this robo-call to help reelect him to Congress.

> This is Senator John McCain. I'm calling to urge you to support my friend, Representative Rick Renzi for Congress. Rick has represented the first district of Arizona with tenacity, honesty, and integrity beyond reproach.[10]

Beyond reproach? After the FBI raided Renzi's house in

April 2007, he resigned his seat on the House Intelligence Committee. Even so, McCain added Renzi to his National Leadership Team and made him a cochair of his Arizona Leadership Team for his presidential campaign.

This wasn't Renzi's first brush with the feds. During his first run for the House in 2002, his campaign finance report raised so much suspicion that the Federal Election Commission (FEC) conducted an audit. It found that Renzi overstated his cash on hand by $64,000, forgot to list the occupations and employers of two hundred contributors, and used $369,000 in loans from "corporate funds" for his campaign.[11]

Unfortunately for Renzi, that last bit is illegal, but the FEC never followed up on this charge. I know. It's shocking that an agency under the Bush administration passed on an investigation of a Republican. It did, however, issue a hefty $1,000 fine to Renzi in 2005 for underreporting campaign donations.

The FBI took a look at Renzi the following year. Renzi's father is an executive vice-president of ManTech Corporation, which provides generous contributions to Renzi junior. Renzi junior sponsored legislation to provide daddy's firm with hundreds of thousands of dollars in contracts in November 2003. The FBI opened an official inquiry just before the 2006 midterm election.[12]

Some of Renzi's business dealings have attracted the wrong kind of attention, too. In October 2005, Renzi sponsored a bill involving some acreage owned by James

Sandlin, who had generously bought out Renzi's interest in a real estate development business. The bill stipulated that Sandlin's acreage would be swapped for a federally owned tract. As it turned out, a developer wanted to build near that tract. A week later Sandlin sold his land for $4.5 million.[13] Two years later, it came out that Sandlin had paid Renzi an additional $200,000 that Renzi failed to report on his financial disclosure forms.[14] The federal attorney looking into this case, Paul Charlton, happened to be one of the eight prosecutors purged by the Bush administration's Department of Justice.

In February 2008, Renzi was indicted for extortion, wire fraud, and money laundering stemming from his land swap as well as for conspiracy to "embezzle and misappropriate client premiums to fund his congressional campaign."[15]

As Renzi went down in flames, McCain remained unusually circumspect for a campaign finance crusader. He stated that he "doesn't know enough of the details" to pass judgment and that "Renzi would probably step down as cochair of his Arizona campaign."[16] Renzi is now absent from McCain's campaign website, but according to one report, he's still in McCain's prayers. Asked if Renzi would continue to work for the campaign, McCain said, "Look, Rick obviously has got great difficulties now. I know nothing about his case. He's in my prayers. He's in my prayers. And that's all I'm going to say. All this stuff will come out."[17] Elsewhere, McCain said, "I feel for the family; as you know, he has 12 children."[18] That should console all

the parents and children who rely on the State Children's
Health Insurance Program (SCHIP), the federal program
that McCain voted not to expand.

Another McCain ally is former campaign manager Terry
Nelson. Nelson was let go because he wasn't performing
well, not because of his role in at least three Republican
scandals: Tom DeLay's money laundering schemes in
Texas, the phone jamming scandal perpetrated in 2002 to
help Senator John Sununu win an open-seat Senate race
against then-Governor Jeanne Shaheen, and the various
doings of Jack Abramoff.[19]

Nelson was the man who approved the racist advertise-
ments used by the Republican National Committee against
Congressman Harold Ford Jr. in his attempt to become a
U.S. Senator from Tennessee in 2006. To play on white
fears of miscegenation (a longtime GOP ploy), Nelson implied that Ford was bedding young white women. The ads
were so offensive that Wal-Mart told Nelson's firm it would
never again produce Wal-Mart's advertising campaigns.

Bob Allen's record pales by comparison. In July 2007,
the former cochair of McCain's Florida campaign was arrested in the Veteran's Memorial Park bathroom in Titus-
ville, Florida. He was charged with soliciting sex from an
undercover police officer for $20.[20] He resigned following
his conviction, but only after first declaring his innocence
and then blaming an African-American cop. It seems one
of the police officers was a "pretty stocky black guy," which
scared Allen, so he felt required to sexually proposition
him in a bathroom.[21]

FRIENDS IN GOVERNMENT

As his relationship with Renzi suggests, McCain's friends in government can be just as shady as his campaign staff and donors. He has campaigned for and been endorsed by one former congressman and another current one—J.D. Hayworth of Arizona and Steve LaTourette of Ohio—who had close ties to former lobbyist Jack Abramoff. Hayworth has spent $200,000 in campaign funds (left over from an unsuccessful bid for office in 2006) on legal fees to fend off a federal indictment for his role in Abramoff's scheme to bilk Native American tribes.[22] LaTourette wrote a letter to the General Services Administration to encourage it to assist an Abramoff associate, "an Indian tribe."[23]

LaTourette is the only one of these three not currently stamping license plates for the state. But he has made up for that by distinguishing himself in his private life. The married congressman was secretly living with his former chief of staff, who had become a lobbyist and later became his wife. By day, she lobbied his committee (Transportation) for her clients; by night, she was presumably making a more personal pitch to him.[24] Maybe this is why LaTourette earned the sobriquet "No Altar Boy" from *Washingtonian* magazine when it polled Capitol Hill staff members on a variety of categories in October 2004.[25]

There appears to be no political marriage John McCain won't endure if it will get him to the White House. Consider this: McCain was scheduled to raise funds for NRCC Chairman Tom Reynolds in 2006, after it was discovered that Reynolds had tried to cover up Congressman Mark Foley's role in sending sexually explicit messages to Senate pages.[26] At the last minute, when the uproar became so loud McCain could finally hear it over his straight talk, he canceled.

Another McCain "friend" is former Senator Phil Gramm of Texas. Known as an appendage of the banking industry when he served in the Senate, Gramm was responsible for blocking efforts to pass legislation that would make it easier to expose money-laundering efforts by terrorists. President Clinton had proposed the reform in light of the Oklahoma City bombing in 1995.

In 2006, McCain supported for reelection to the House the likes of Jim Nussle (R-IA), Steve Chabot (R-OH), and Gil Gutknecht (R-MN), and to the Senate, a fellow who exudes racism and corporate scandal—George Allen (R-VA).[27] Nussle, Chabot, and Gutknecht opposed his efforts at campaign-finance reform, so in backing them, McCain broke his pledge not to offer assistance to those who would stymie reform. Allen, who is best known for using the racial slur "Macaca," liked to hang a noose in his office when he was younger. The Associated Press reported that he "failed to tell Congress about stock options he got for his work as a director of a high-tech company" and that he "asked the Army to help another business that gave him similar options."[28] Yet McCain decided that Allen was the best person to introduce him for his speech at the Conservative Political Action Conference (CPAC) in February 2008.

Where is the John McCain we thought we knew during the 2000 presidential campaign? McCain 3.0 has new friends, which is often a good thing. In this case, these friends have done nothing to advance McCain's reforms. But they've done a lot to fund or otherwise advance his political career.

EIGHT

Sex, Life, and Videotape

IN 2000 MCCAIN WENT TO VIRGINIA during its presidential primary and articulated a sentiment many Americans agreed with. "Neither party," he said, "should be defined by pandering to the outer reaches of American politics and the agents of intolerance." He went on to identify Pat Robertson and Jerry Falwell as such agents—and he did so in their home state.

We know what those men have stood for over the years — an America where fundamentalist teachings become policy (or at least the guiding principles) on homosexuality, abortion, and science. Running against the puerile George W. Bush, McCain came off as the grownup, the maverick, the guy who called them as he saw them.

The story of what has happened to that man—in a sound bite, in a heartbeat—is an American travesty. On a range of social issues, McCain has continually ducked the tough questions and pandered to some of the least tolerant forces in American society.

LOVING FALWELL

McCain has decided—coolly, and with utmost calculation—that he needs the support of the very groups he
stood up to in 2000. He needs their money, their energy,
their support—and yes, their blessing. Throwing previously stated principles out the window, McCain praised
Reverend Falwell on *Meet The Press* on April 2, 2006,
and went on to deliver a commencement address at the
Reverend's Liberty University six weeks later.[1]

Exactly who and what was McCain praising? Reverend
Falwell is no longer with us, but his words live on. Here are
some of them on the subject of 9/11.

> I really believe that the pagans, and the abortionists, and
> the feminists, and the gays and the lesbians who are actively
> trying to make that an alternative lifestyle, the ACLU,
> People for the American Way—all of them who have tried
> to secularize America—I point the finger in their face and
> say, "You helped this happen."[2]

In Kingsport, Tennessee, Falwell shared his thoughts on
the Antichrist: "[W]hen he appears during the Tribulation
period he will be a full-grown counterfeit of Christ. Of
course he'll be Jewish. Of course he'll pretend to be
Christ."[3] Finally, there was Falwell's outing of Tinky Winky
of *Teletubbies* fame. The sharp-eyed preacher was able to
warn America of a homosexual predator. "He is purple,
the gay-pride color; and his antenna is shaped like a tri-
angle, the gay-pride symbol."[4]

For his 2008 presidential run, McCain won't have to face the question of whether to break bread with Falwell, who died in 2007. But he will have to avert a mutiny among Christian conservatives who favored Mike Huckabee and Mitt Romney in the primaries. On learning of Falwell's death, McCain eulogized him as "a man of distinguished accomplishment who devoted his life to serving his faith and country."[5] It was a start.

CRAZY BASE LAND

Falwell isn't the only figure on the extreme right with whom McCain has sought a rapprochement. When Christian Right leader and Focus on the Family founder Dr. James Dobson said on his radio show that he would not support a McCain presidential candidacy "under any circumstances," McCain responded with sweet talk: "I'm obviously disappointed and I'd like to continue and have a dialogue with Dr. Dobson and other members of the community."[6]

McCain also was escorted around a Christian broadcasters' convention by the Reverend Patrick Mahoney of the Christian Defense Coalition. Mahoney is a former member of Operation Rescue, which tries to block access to abortion clinics by forming human chains and castigating or threatening women who try to pass them. Mahoney formed the Christian Defense Coalition specifically to keep Terri Schiavo on a feeding tube.[7] Doing so clashed with her husband's wishes, court rulings, and the opinions of two-thirds of Americans. McCain took Mahoney's position, despite the specter of government intrusion into family life that probably would have appalled his ex-mentor, Barry Goldwater.

McCain has developed an increasingly solid relationship with the reverends Richard Land and John Hagee. Reverend Land has made it his business to threaten television stations with boycotts if their programs feature gay couples. Land has offered support for McCain, telling Chris Wallace of Fox News that he could support McCain, in spite of his divorce, because of his status as a war hero.[8] But Land was also careful to say that "many evangelicals find him unpredictable, they don't know where he'll come down on an issue."[9]

McCain met with San Antonio televangelist John Hagee to discuss their shared "commitment to the state of Israel."[10] Here's how journalist Max Blumenthal summarized Hagee's views on the Middle East.

> The only way to defeat the Iranian evildoers, [Hagee] says, is a full-scale military assault. "The coming nuclear showdown with Iran is a certainty," Hagee wrote this year in the Pentecostal magazine *Charisma*. "Israel and America must confront Iran's nuclear ability and willingness to destroy Israel with nuclear weapons. For Israel to wait is to risk committing national suicide."[11]

McCain has refused to disavow Hagee and his views, despite the fact that Hagee has called Catholicism "The Great Whore" and offers the full-blown version of the End Times in his apocalyptic bestseller, *Jerusalem Countdown*. In

fact, McCain said he was "proud" to receive Hagee's endorsement.[12] Maybe that's what our country needs right
now: a little more Armageddon in our foreign policy.

Given all the talk about his moderate views, McCain
has a long list of right-wing extremist friends. In the 2006
Republican primary for Ohio governor, McCain endorsed
Ohio Secretary of State Ken Blackwell over the more moderate Attorney General Jim Petro. Blackwell is a hard-core
conservative; he campaigned (successfully) for a state constitutional ban on same-sex marriage, is a big-time pro-gun
politician, and is against abortion unless the mother's life
is threatened.

There are also questions of voter suppression in Blackwell's background, particularly in light of the sparse
number of voting machines in liberal Ohio districts on
election day in 2004. These questions were complicated
by Blackwell's investment in Diebold, the company that
supplied the touch-screen machines on Blackwell's orders. Blackwell is also closely tied to Reverend Rod Parsely
of Columbus, Ohio; together they have worked with the
Ohio Restoration Project, which calls for "tearing down
the boundaries between church and state."[13] In the end,
Blackwell lost the general election in a landslide. But it
wasn't for lack of support on McCain's part.

Then there's Falwell. When McCain decided to visit
Falwell's university, Jon Stewart asked McCain on the *Daily
Show* if he was entering "crazy base land." McCain sheep-
ishly admitted he was doing just that.[14] This is how the ac-
tual exchange went.

Stewart: I feel it's a condoning of Falwell's crazy making, to some extent, to have you go down there. It strikes me as something you wouldn't normally do.

McCain: I'm going there to speak to the students at his invitation. I can assure you that the message will be the same as I give everywhere.

Stewart: You don't think it helps reassert Falwell as the voice for a certain group of people—say evangelicals of the Christian Right. Isn't it the kind of thing if you don't go there it helps keep marginalizing guys like that? Or do I misunderstand politics? Why do I feel I'm about to get grounded?

McCain: Listen, I love coming on your show. Young people all over America watch it. I love to travel around the country and speak at colleges and universities. They're all parts of the Republican Party. I respect them. I may disagree with them.

Stewart: Are you going into crazy base world?

McCain: I'm afraid so.

Stewart: When you see Falwell, do you feel vomit in the back of your throat? . . . What does it feel like?

McCain: I'll give him your love.[15]

That was slightly different than what McCain told Larry King less than a year earlier: "I admire the religious right for the dedication and zeal they put into the political process."[16] McCain's broad acceptance of the Christian Right as "having a legitimate role to play in the Republican Party" stands in stark opposition to his earlier claims that the Christian Right had a "corrupting influence" on the GOP.[17]

This is just one of those areas where McCain is going to have to agree to disagree—with himself.

LIFE: TAKES ONE AND TWO

On August 20, 1999, McCain had this to say about abortion to an audience at Commonwealth Club of California.

> I'd love to see a point where (*Roe vs. Wade*) is irrelevant, and could be repealed because abortion is no longer necessary. But certainly in the short term, or even the long term, I would not support repeal of *Roe vs. Wade*, which would then force X number of women in America to (undergo) illegal and dangerous operations.[18]

Two days later, on CNN's *Late Edition* and as reported in the *Washington Post*, McCain said he would "ultimately" support the repeal of *Roe v. Wade*, but not in the short term. The *Post* quoted the senator's response to a query during the CNN interview: "We all know, and it's obvious, that if we repeal *Roe v. Wade* tomorrow, thousands of young American women would be performing illegal and dangerous operations."[19]

McCain was also quoted as saying that if his daughter got pregnant, it would be her decision whether or not to carry the baby to term. Later, he amended this to "a family decision." Either way, it's a pro-choice position.

But in 2006, McCain declared that he's not only completely in favor of overturning *Roe v. Wade* but also that he would support a Constitutional amendment to ban abortion in virtually all circumstances.[20] In a May 2007 appearance on *Meet the Press*, McCain said he has "always been pro-life, unchanging and unwavering."[21] As for worrying about forcing women to undergo dangerous and illegal operations, he wasn't thinking about that when he declared his support for South Dakota's proposed ban on abortion—a measure so draconian that it would have forced women who had been the victims of rape or incest to bear the progeny of their attacker.[22] South Dakota voters rejected the measure in 2006.[23]

Even after all of McCain's pandering, however, dedicated pro-lifers know that his heart isn't with them. Instead, they see him as a flip-flopper (at least on this issue), a view they share with pro-choice voters. Earlier this year, former Pennsylvania Senator and pro-life firebrand Rick Santorum was asked whom he would support in the GOP primaries. His answer: anybody but McCain. Santorum made the common but oblique reference to McCain's temper, saying, "I don't think he has the temperament and leadership ability to move the country in the right direction." But then he added a flourish: "He may be pro-life, but I served with him for twelve years, and I know how pro-life he is."[24]

Conservative media consultant and pro-life activist Joe Gigante had the same reaction. He should know, having served as director of public relations and spokesman for the American Life League. He told me, "When it is politically expedient, McCain becomes far more conservative. Conservative voters need to beware." As far as Gigante is concerned, the only thing that can be said about McCain on the issue of abortion is that he is "consistently inconsistent."[25]

For all of his anti-abortion posturing, McCain has done little to reduce unwanted pregnancies in the first place. In March 2005, he voted against the funding of education and contraceptives to reduce teen pregnancy.[26]

WAR ON CONDOMS

McCain is remarkably unclear on another urgent issue: reducing the rate of HIV infection in Africa. In 2007, he hemmed and hawed during an interview with the *New York Times* on the question of condom distribution there. Here's part of the transcript.

Reporter: Should U.S. taxpayer money go to places like Africa to fund contraception to prevent AIDS?

Mr. McCain: Well I think it's a combination. The guy I really respect on this is Dr. Coburn. He believes—and I was just reading the thing he wrote—that you should do what you can to encourage abstinence where there is going to be sexual activity. Where that doesn't succeed, than he thinks that we should employ contraceptives as well. But I agree with him that the first priority is on abstinence. I look to people like Dr. Coburn. I'm not very wise on it.

(Mr. McCain turns to take a question on Iraq, but a moment later looks back to the reporter who asked him about AIDS.)

Mr. McCain: I haven't thought about it. Before I give you an answer, let me think . . . Let me think about it a little bit because I never got a question about it before. I don't know if I would use taxpayers' money for it.

Q: What about grants for sex education in the United States? Should they include instructions about using contraceptives? Or should it be Bush's policy, which is just abstinence?

Mr. McCain: (Long pause) Ahhh. I think I support the president's policy.

Q: So no contraception, no counseling on contraception. Just abstinence. Do you think contraceptives help stop the spread of HIV?

Mr. McCain: (Long pause) You've stumped me.

Q: I mean, I think you'd probably agree it probably does help stop it?

Mr. McCain: (Laughs) Are we on the Straight Talk Express? I'm not informed enough on it. Let me find out. You know, I'm sure I've taken a position on it in the past. I have to find out what my position was. Brian, would you find out what my position is on contraception—I'm sure I'm opposed to government spending on it, I'm sure I support the president's policies on it.

Q: But you would agree that condoms do stop the spread of sexually transmitted diseases. Would you say: "No, we're not going to distribute them," knowing that?

Mr. McCain: (twelve-second pause) Get me Coburn's thing, ask Weaver to get me Coburn's paper that he just gave me in the last couple of days. I've never gotten into these issues before.[27]

At least McCain had the wit to joke about condoms on the Straight Talk Express. But this exchange is where McCain finally lost political analyst Steve Benen.

He doesn't know if he believes condoms are effective in preventing the spread of HIV? He's been a member of Congress for twenty-four years, has participated in thousands of policy hearings, and has voted on hundreds of bills relating to public health. Now that he's running for president, McCain literally has no idea what he thinks about something as simple as condoms and HIV? Please.

I was particularly fond of the "I have to find out what my position was" remark. Someone can ask him an extremely simple question, but before he answers it, McCain wants to check to make sure he believes what he thinks he believes. "Would you find out what my position is on contraception?" Here's a wacky idea, Senator, why don't you just tell us what you actually think?[28]

SENATOR, HEAL THYSELF

McCain's policy floundering is especially ironic given that he is still regarded in some quarters as a Western libertarian in the Goldwater tradition. Matt Welch doesn't buy it. He wrote a feature article for the April 2007 edition of *Reason Magazine*, a libertarian publication, called "Be Afraid of President McCain: The Frightening Mind of an Authoritarian Maverick."

Welch's article has many interesting bits. Buried in the middle is this claim: "John spent his teens and twenties constantly flirting with disciplinary disaster by breaking every drinking and curfew rule on the books, concentrating more on Brazilian heiresses and Florida strippers than on his aviating skills."[29] To his credit, McCain has been honest about this period of his life. But one would think that his

candor makes it harder to lecture kids on avoiding pre-
marital sex.

Evidently not. McCain has hopped aboard the Abstinence
Express, which has other problems besides McCain's low
credibility. As James Wagoner, president of Advocates for
Youth, has put it, "After 10 years and $1.5 billion in pub-
lic funds, these failed abstinence-only-until-marriage programs will go down as an ideological boondoggle of his-
toric proportions." Wagoner goes on.

> The tragedy is not simply the waste of taxpayer dollars, it is
> the damage done to the young people who have been on
> the receiving end of distorted, inaccurate information about
> condoms and birth control. We have been promoting
> ignorance in the era of AIDS, and that's not just bad public
> health policy, its bad ethics.[30]

That tragedy didn't stop McCain from spreading the
abstinence gospel among teenagers in South Carolina.
McCain spokesman Trey Walker made sure to bask in the
glow of the senator's pro-chastity position. Walker proclaimed, "Senator McCain has a long legislative record of
supporting abstinence-based initiatives in the U.S. Senate,"
and "He thinks that abstinence is healthier and should be
promoted in our society for young people."[31] As a young
man, McCain didn't have much use for it, but that's another matter.

Public figures take a chance when they climb onto the
moral pedestal. For one thing, their pronouncements in-
vite scrutiny of their own private lives. McCain is no dif-

ferent, and his life has taken many twists and turns. Sadly, when McCain returned to his wife Carol after he was released by his Vietnamese captors, she had been disabled in a car accident. It was, no doubt, another tough period for them as a couple.

One wonders if McCain 3.0 would approve of the way the young McCain handled that difficulty. McCain's marital infidelities have been given relatively little media attention, though he courted the woman who became his second wife while he was still married to Carol. According to Nicholas Kristof, writing in the *New York Times,* "Mr. McCain has acknowledged running around with women and accepted responsibility for the breakup of the marriage, without going into details."[32] Steve Benen added more detail in a piece for the *Washington Monthly.*

> McCain divorced his wife, who had raised their three
> children while he was imprisoned in Vietnam, then launched
> his political career with his new wife's family money. In 2000
> McCain managed to deflect media questioning about his
> first marriage with a deft admission of responsibility for its
> failure.[33]

Perhaps wary of answering to Republican voters on this matter, McCain took a preemptive stance during a campaign appearance in March 2007. "I would like to see this campaign conducted on past record and ambition for the future . . . I would hope that gossip—or, quote, 'family issues'—would not enter into this campaign."[34]

None of this prevented Senator McCain from voting to

impeach President Bill Clinton for lying about a marital
indiscretion.

THE NATURAL EVOLUTION OF INTELLIGENT DESIGN

Shifting now to less personal issues, let's consider another
conservative touchstone. Where does Senator McCain
stand on the teaching of evolution? Back in 2000, McCain
stated his belief that this was a matter that states should
decide. More recently he claimed in a Republican presidential candidate debate that he personally believes in
evolution but sees "the hand of God" involved, too.

On this issue, McCain's clarity is refreshing: he's on both
sides. When asked by the *Arizona Star* in 2005 whether intelligent design should be taught in science class, McCain
said, "There's enough scientists that believe it does. I'm
not a scientist. This is something that I think all points of
view should be presented."[35] In 2006, ABC News reported,
"Senator McCain is now advocating 'intelligent design,' a
form of scientific creationism, which argues an intelligent
designer played a role in the evolution of life on earth. He
wants it taught alongside evolution theory."[36] But in Aspen
that same year, McCain said of intelligent design, "Should
it be taught as a science class? Probably not."[37]

Evidently, McCain's position is still evolving.

MCCAIN'S GAY NINETIES

In 1999 McCain was the GOP candidate who was the most
gay friendly. *Slate* reporter Jacob Weisberg recalled how

McCain told him in an interview in the mid-1990s that having gay staffers had "sensitized" him to the issue.[38]

During that election, McCain agreed to sit down with the
premier GOP gay advocacy organization, the Log Cabin
Republicans, which President Bush pointedly refused to
do. McCain didn't make any promises, but many of the
group's members supported McCain vocally and financially
thereafter, endorsing a potential candidacy in 2004.[39]

Since then, however, McCain has demonstrated impressive verbal gymnastics on the issue of gay rights. That includes clever caveats, position switching, and the artful
avoidance of straight talk. His maneuvers have created
some fun television moments.

In October 2006, *Hardball* host Chris Matthews asked
McCain if he supported gay marriage. McCain said, "I think
gay marriage should be allowed if there's a ceremony kind
of thing if you want to call it that. I don't have any problem
with that." When the show resumed after a commercial
break, McCain hijacked a question on a completely different topic and interjected, "I think private ceremonies are
fine. I do not think gay marriage should be legal."[40]

The next month, McCain was a guest on *This Week
with George Stephanopoulos*. Stephanopoulos asked McCain
whether he was against civil unions for gay couples. "No, I'm
not," McCain replied. A few minutes later, Stephanopoulos
tried again. "So you're for civil unions?" "No," McCain
said. Neither for nor against civil unions, McCain went on
to clarify his position. He was against "discrimination," and
he referred obliquely to certain partnerships qualifying for
things like "hospital visits."[41]

Yet the state constitutional amendment that he stumped for in Arizona that year would have banned not only gay marriage but also *all benefits for domestic partners*—including hospital visits. In July 2004, McCain also took the position that a federal amendment was unnecessary because the 1996 Defense of Marriage Act (DOMA) already allowed states to refuse to recognize gay marriages sanctioned in other states. For that reason, the federal constitutional amendment was "un-Republican."[42] Three months earlier, he had told Jerry Falwell he would support such an amendment if state constitutional bans were struck down by the courts.[43]

THE RACE ISSUE

Race is one of the hot-button social issues of our time. As someone whose ancestors owned slaves and fought on the side of the Confederacy, McCain might have gone out of his way to stake out a clear and progressive position. Instead, McCain is a mixed bag. Early in his career, he voted against making Reverend Martin Luther King, Jr.'s birthday a federal holiday. In 2000, however, he attacked then-Governor Bush for speaking at Bob Jones University, calling the university's ban on interracial dating "idiotic and cruel." But when McCain decided to run for president again, he said he would be happy to speak at Bob Jones University.[44]

Nothing reveals McCain's contortionism better than his various positions on the Confederate flag. In September

1999, McCain said that choosing whether to fly the Confederate flag "should be left to the states."[45] In January 2000, he proclaimed, "The Confederate flag is offensive in many, many ways, as we all know. It's a symbol of racism and slavery."[46] Three days later, he said, "Personally, I see the flag as a symbol of heritage."[47]

It's a long journey from "racism and slavery" to "heritage" in only three days. So it wasn't surprising to learn that it was a journey McCain never actually took. He made this clear in an April 2000 speech in South Carolina. McCain told the mostly supportive crowd, "I feared that if I answered honestly, I could not win the South Carolina primary . . . So I chose to compromise my principles. I broke my promise to always tell the truth."[48]

McCain received a standing ovation for this belated admission, but one man in the audience held out. Here's how the Stephen Holmes of the *New York Times* described the scene.

> One person who did not join in the acclaim for Mr. McCain was Jake Knotts, a state Republican representative from Lexington County outside Columbia who sat in stony silence while others applauded. Mr. Knotts was one of the few Republican legislators who supported Mr. McCain in the primary. He is also a flag supporter who said he had pressed Mr. McCain in the campaign on his true feelings about the Confederate icon.
>
> "Yes, I'm disappointed in him, very disappointed in him," Mr. Knotts said to reporters after the speech. "I'm not only disappointed, I'm ashamed of him. I'm ashamed that he lied

to the people of South Carolina in order to further his political career."[49]

Many Americans would have supported a repudiation of the South's overall record on race. But what about McCain's new friends in the evangelical community? Four years after the Warren Court ordered the nation's public schools to desegregate in the landmark *Brown v. Board of Education* decision, Jerry Falwell took to the pulpit to deliver his sermon, "Segregation or Integration, Which?"

> If Chief Justice Warren and his associates had known God's word and had desired to do the Lord's will, I am quite confident that the 1954 decision would never have been made. The facilities should be separate. When God has drawn a line of distinction, we should not attempt to cross that line.

Falwell went on to announce that integration "will destroy our race eventually. In one northern city," he warned, "a pastor friend of mine tells me that a couple of opposite race live next door to his church as man and wife."[50] Falwell also called the 1964 Civil Rights Act "civil wrongs," Bishop Desmond Tutu a "phony," and the Reverend Martin Luther King, Jr. a Communist. Falwell was also a big fan of the apartheid-era government of South Africa.

This might all be ancient history, at least by the standards of American politics. But consider McCain's quite recent decision to hire Terry Nelson as his campaign manager for his 2008 presidential bid. In his role as advisor to the Republican National Committee during the 2006 midterm elections, Nelson produced the now-infamous television ad attacking Democratic Senate candidate Harold Ford Jr. by playing on racial fears of black men lusting after white women.[51]

On a wide range of social issues, McCain has consistently chosen political expediency over principle. His flip-flops have kept him in the game, but they reveal a widening gap between image and reality, and perhaps what kind of president he would make. Eagle-eyed conservatives are watching that gap. Moderate-minded independents fail to do so at their peril.

NINE

Torture, Taxes, and the Teeming Masses

A profile in courage can become a profile in unrestrained
ambition, says former Reagan White House chief of staff
Ken Duberstein, who was one of the few G.O.P. establishment
figures to support McCain's 2000 presidential campaign.
"He has to remember who his friends are and not spend
his integrity on one-night stands with those who will never
fully trust him."
> —Former Reagan White House Chief of Staff Ken Duberstein
> on McCain, *Time* Magazine, December 10, 2006

JOHN MCCAIN WITHSTOOD five and a half years of
torture and brutal imprisonment at the hands of the
North Vietnamese, and remained strong and unbreak-
able throughout. But when it came to giving the Bush administration what it wanted, he set aside his own beliefs
about the efficacy and ethics of torture and sponsored a
bill in December 2005 that offers two forms of protection
to torturers. Remarkably, he did all this while preserving
his image as a man who, having been the victim of torture, remains steadfastly against it. But the details of the

Detainee Treatment Act, known as the "McCain bill" and signed by George W. Bush, tell a different story. It's complex, which may be one reason the media cling to a more simplistic—and distorted—version.

In November 2001, a man named Ibn Sheikh al-Libi, a suspected paramilitary trainer for Al Qaeda, was arrested in Pakistan after fleeing Afghanistan. In January 2002, al-Libi, while under torture aboard the *USS Bataan,* confessed to knowing that Al Qaeda had participated in the development of weapons of mass destruction in Iraq. Thirteen months later, Colin Powell repeated al-Libi's claims as part of the American justification for going to war with Iraq and toppling Saddam Hussein's regime. Thus the fruits of torture became a crucial factor in determining our foreign policy.

Most experts say that the information obtained under torture is unreliable. From his own experience, McCain certainly knew that. After all, he gave his interrogators very little information, and much of it (for example, the identities of the Green Bay Packers offensive line) was a mite misleading.

But the invasion of Iraq was based on just such bogus information—not only from the tortured prisoner al-Libi (who later recanted), but also from an Iraqi exile, Ahmad Chalabi, who was subsequently proven to be anything but reliable himself. They both told Bush administration officials what they wanted to hear. But international outrage over torture, especially after the photographs from Abu Ghraib prison appeared, made it necessary for these officials to respond. Keep in mind the circumstances: the administration had justified the invasion of Iraq with information gleaned from torture, the occupation of Iraq wasn't going well, torture is against U.S. and international law, and the lawsuits were piling up like cord wood.[1]

TORTURE IN THE COURTS

In one of those lawsuits, *Rasul v. Bush*, the Supreme Court established that the U.S. court system has the authority to decide whether foreign nationals (non–U.S. citizens) held in Guantanamo Bay were rightfully imprisoned. This presented a problem for the government, which had detained as many as fourteen thousand people in connection with the hunt for Al Qaeda. Also, the rest of the world was beginning to think that these prisoners were subjected to ill treatment and torture in violation of international law.

Another case involved Salim Hamdan, a Yemeni citizen arrested during the invasion of Afghanistan. Hamdan admitted that he was Osama bin Laden's driver and bodyguard. Held in Guantanamo, Hamdan was supposed to be tried before a military commission for conspiracy and material support for terrorism. He contended that the military commissions violated both the Uniform Code of Military Justice and the Geneva Conventions. A district court (Judge John Roberts, now chief justice of the Supreme Court, presiding) ruled against him in *Hamdan v. Rumsfeld*, but Hamdan appealed to the Supreme Court, which decided to hear the case.

Anticipating defeat, the Bush administration took pre-emptive action. With John McCain's support, Bush signed the Detainee Treatment Act of 2005. The new law took some interrogation options away from the military, but its fine print also took away the right for prisoners like Hamdan to challenge their detention. It also indemnified (in effect, excused) torturers who may not have known they were breaking the law. Bush claimed he didn't like "the McCain language," but signed it into law anyway. [2]

By passing its own Detainee Treatment Act, Congress may have been hoping to persuade the Court of the wisdom of the White House position. It didn't work. In June 2006, the Court upheld the right of prisoners of war to contest the grounds of their detention in a U.S. court and declared the military commissions unconstitutional unless sanctioned by an act of Congress. It also declared that the Geneva Conventions applied to "unlawful enemy combatants," not just prisoners of war.

So the Bush administration went back to work. Four months after the court decided *Hamdan v. Rumsfeld*, Bush signed the Military Commissions Act of 2006. That law prevented prisoners from challenging their detention. It also stated, "No alien unlawful enemy combatant subject to trial by military commission under this chapter may invoke the Geneva Conventions as a source of rights."

John McCain was happy. Here's what he said in an official statement:

Simply put, this legislation ensures that we respect our obligations under Geneva, recognizes the President's

constitutional authority to interpret treaties, and brings
accountability and transparency to the process of interpretation by ensuring that the executive's interpretation is
made public. I would note that there has been opposition to
this legislation from some quarters, including the *New York
Times* editorial page. Without getting into a point-by-point
rebuttal here on the floor, I would simply say that I have
been reading the Congressional Record trying to find the
bill that page so vociferously denounced. The hyperbolic
attack is aimed not at any bill this body is today debating,
nor even at the administration's original position. I can only
presume that some would prefer that Congress simply
ignore the Hamdan decision, and pass no legislation at all.
That, I suggest to my colleagues, would be a travesty.[3]

The logic is spooky. The bill that revokes Geneva protections "respects our obligations under Geneva." Presidents
don't have to follow treaties like Geneva; rather, they
only have to make their "interpretations" of them public.
Critics who fault the new law are living in la-la land; the
only choice in the real world is between a terrible new law
and the perfectly adequate (if completely ignored) laws
we have now.

The spookiness wasn't lost on the *Washington Post*, which
had this to say.

In short, it's hard to credit the statement by Sen. John
McCain (R-Ariz.) yesterday that "there's no doubt that the
integrity and letter and spirit of the Geneva Conventions
have been preserved." In effect, the agreement means that

U.S. violations of international human rights law can continue as long as Mr. Bush is president, with Congress's tacit assent. If they do, America's standing in the world will continue to suffer, as will the fight against terrorism.[4]

The timing was precious. Bush pushed the new law through just before the midterm elections rebuked the GOP for an illegal, unjustified, and disastrous war. Rumsfeld, the named party in many detainee charges, would resign in November. But Bush had already achieved his purpose—with McCain's help.

The same *Washington Post* piece noted that achievement.

A senior administration official, who spoke on the condition of anonymity, said in an interview that Bush essentially got what he asked for in a different formulation that allows both sides to maintain that their concerns were addressed. "We kind of take the scenic route, but we get there," the official said.[5]

The new law mostly dealt with what military interrogators could and couldn't do. But what about the intelligence agencies? In February 2008, McCain voted against a bill that would require the CIA to abide by the interrogation restrictions in the Army Field Manual. The bill passed but faces a likely veto by President Bush, who believes, as does McCain, that the CIA should have the flexibility to use other tactics. Does that include the infamous "waterboarding"? Bush refuses to be hemmed in by anyone else's definition of what constitutes the "cruel, inhumane and degrading treatment" described in the Military Commissions Act. McCain's vote indicates that he supports Bush's position.

TAXES OF EVIL

Another issue where one McCain has run up against another is taxes. When running for president in 2000, McCain claimed that candidate Bush's plan was skewed toward the wealthy. After the campaign, he and Lincoln Chafee were the only Republican senators to oppose President Bush's signature tax package in 2001.[6] McCain claimed he couldn't vote to cut tax rates for the wealthy "at the expense of middle-class Americans."[7] In 2003, McCain decried tax cuts during wartime and voted against Bush's second tax package.[8] Strong, principled stuff.

But when McCain began to position himself for another run at the White House, he changed his tune. His earlier opposition to tax cuts, he explained, was based on his sense that the cuts weren't accompanied by sufficient spending cuts. Then he jumped enthusiastically on the tax-cut bandwagon, voting in 2006 to extend portions of the Bush tax cuts.[9] If those tax cuts aren't made permanent, he said, it would be the equivalent of a tax increase, and "I've never voted for a tax increase in 24 years."[10] (In fact, he voted for a tobacco tax increase in 1998.[11]) Granted, he's no Mike Huckabee, who would abolish the IRS altogether. But he's not the John McCain we knew in 2001, either.

McCain 3.0 has also become a GOP leader in the effort
to repeal the estate tax. Not too long ago (2005, for those
of you taking notes), he recoiled at the thought of working
for its repeal.

> In the last year we have approved legislation containing
> billions and billions of dollars—in pork-barrel projects,
> huge tax breaks for the wealthy, and a corporate tax bill
> estimated to cost $180 billion. This is a far cry from sacrifice.
> Young Americans are putting their lives on the line to serve
> their country in Iraq, while those who are whining about the
> estate tax are fighting to keep every last cent. A time of war
> is no time to eliminate the estate tax.[12]

"Whining" is a strong word to apply to your colleagues
and their constituents. In March 2006, McCain issued a
statement indicating that he might be willing to reduce
the estate tax. Eventually, then–Senate Majority Leader Bill
Frist (R-TN) allowed McCain to take charge of an effort to
reduce or repeal the tax—the very tax that McCain's idol,
Teddy Roosevelt, had enacted to ameliorate vast dispari-
ties in wealth.[13] McCain had become whiner-in-chief.

With the tax issue, McCain has perfected the seemingly
impossible feat of resisting cuts and arguing for their per-
manence, as well as ridiculing repeal of the estate tax and
endorsing it. In the process, he also did something else
that, in retrospect, may have been unwise: he risked caus-
ing distrust among American conservatives and damaged
his straight-talking reputation cherished for so long by
independent voters.

PORK: THE OTHER WHITE MEAT

McCain has long spoken with missionary zeal about the need to eliminate congressional earmarks, the insertion of funding for pet projects into bills. He has taken a "No Pork Pledge," and said that "we're not going to fix this system until we fix earmarks."[14] When asked about lobbying reform during an appearance on *Fox News Sunday* in January 2006—while he still supported such reform—McCain said, "If we don't stop the earmarking, we're not going to stop the abuses of power here in Washington."[15]

This kind of talk was too much for at least one man. Winslow Wheeler spent thirty-one years working for Senate members and at the General Accounting Office (GAO). Still a registered Republican, he worked in the Senate for one Democrat, former Arkansas Senator David Pryor, and three Republicans, all belonging to the traditional center-right wing of the party: the late Senator Jacob Javits of New York, former Senator Nancy Landon Kassebaum of Kansas, and Senator Pete Domenici of New Mexico.

Wheeler isn't exactly someone you'd expect to launch a withering critique of fellow Republicans. But he did, and it raised the ire of a certain senator from Arizona, who helped end Wheeler's career in the Senate.

Wheeler had long noticed McCain's tough talk on pork-barrel spending. In fact, cutting pork from spending bills is one of the planks McCain is running on in 2008—an effort to appeal to conservatives tired of the free-spending Bush years as well as to display his supposed credentials as

a "reformer." But Wheeler hadn't noticed much in the way
of action from McCain. In 2002 he published a short book,
under the pseudonym Spartacus, called *Mr. Smith Is Dead:
No One Stands in the Way as Congress Lards Post—September 11
Defense Bills with Pork*. His purpose was to give McCain "a
kick in the ass."[16]

One of Wheeler's anecdotes is particularly telling. When
Senator Ted Stevens of Alaska was pushing for a $26 bil-
lion Boeing 767 lease that made no economic or strategic
sense, McCain and Phil Gramm offered an amendment
to thwart it. But according to Wheeler, here's what really
happened.

> McCain included a cauterization of it in his "pork buster"
> speech: he called the operating lease "a sweet deal for the
> Boeing Company that I'm sure is the envy of corporate
> lobbyists from one end of K Street to the other." He was
> supported by Sen. Phil Gramm, R-Texas, who said, "I do
> not think I have even seen a proposal that makes less sense
> economically and I have been here for 22 years." Given the
> strong rhetoric, one would expect some strong action, right?
>
> Not exactly. McCain and Gramm did offer an amendment
> to modify the 767 deal. Stevens accepted it without debate.
> He was smart to do so. As he explained to Gramm and
> McCain, the terms of the amendment changed nothing,
> and he would accept it for that reason. The amendment
> was pure cosmetics, but now McCain and Gramm could
> claim they did something.
>
> Shortly after this charade, the Senate passed the bill and

sent it to conference with the House to conform the two bodies' different versions into one.[17]

McCain's response? He got Wheeler fired. According to Wheeler (and a second source who wished to remain anonymous), McCain went to Wheeler's boss, Senator Pete Domenici, as well as other top-ranking Republican staffers, to argue that Wheeler could not be trusted. McCain made it clear, according to Wheeler, that he would be angry if Wheeler were not fired. Problem solved. McCain didn't change his behavior to match his rhetoric—he just got rid of the guy who was willing to call him on it.

After Wheeler and I had discussed these circumstances at some length, he ended our conversation by saying in a foreboding voice, "It's frightening to think of a man with his temperament with all the things a President has at his fingertips—the IRS, CIA, FBI. . . ."[18]

ON IMMIGRATION

Finally, there is the bitterly divisive issue of immigration, on which McCain might seem to be a positive force. After all, he has tried to reach across the aisle to solve the many complex issues involved, and many Republicans have criticized this seemingly commendable effort. But appearances can, once again, be deceiving.

A February 2007 *Vanity Fair* article contains a particularly insightful anecdote regarding McCain's willingness to abandon his beliefs on immigration reform.

A day earlier, in Milwaukee, in front of an audience of more
sympathetic businessmen, McCain had been asked how
debate over the immigration bill was playing politically.
"In the short term, it probably galvanizes our base," he
said. "In the long term, if you alienate the Hispanics, you'll
pay a heavy price." Then he added, unable to help himself,
"By the way, I think the fence is least effective. But I'll build
the goddamned fence if they want it."[19]

In 2006 McCain cosponsored a version of an immigration reform bill with that bête noire of the conservatives,
Senator Ted Kennedy. According to one source who spoke
to me on condition of anonymity, McCain was mostly concerned about creating a labor supply for his business allies. It was Kennedy who made sure many of the worker
protections were included in the bill.

Liberal blogger and author David Sirota echoed a similar theme, quoting McCain's claim that immigrants were
needed for cheap labor.

McCain justified his support for an immigration bill by
claiming that agriculture companies simply can't find
Americans to do the jobs they need done. When told that
people won't do those jobs because the companies pay such
awful wages, McCain claimed that Americans wouldn't want
to pick lettuce for $50 an hour—a line that got him yelled
off the stage.[20]

In the end, the immigration bill never got out of
Congress. According to a senior Senate staff member in-

volved in the immigration negotiations, McCain first delayed his involvement, then backed out of the day-to-day negotiations. He has since shifted to the right to try to appease the Republican base.

The same anonymous source said he didn't know of "anyone besides Lindsay Graham and Joe Lieberman in the Senate who actually liked McCain." That impression is supported by a 2006 poll of Senate staffers in which McCain came in second in the categories of "Show Horse," "Worst Follower," and "Worst Temper."[21] McCain tied for first with Senator Chuck Hagel for "Straightest Shooter," but this was in September 2006, before he began his presidential campaign in earnest.

This source's account is supported by a May 2007 piece for the *Washington Post* titled "Top GOP Hopefuls Keep Distance on Immigration."

> McCain, once the most visible Republican in the fight for immigration reform . . . has handed off day-to-day negotiations on immigration to his staff and to fellow Senate Republicans Jon Kyl (Ariz.) and Lindsey O. Graham (S.C.). In his formal presidential announcement speech in New Hampshire last month, he made no mention of the issue . . . McCain said Sunday on NBC's "Meet the Press" that he is "heavily engaged". . . But a top Senate Democrat said last week that McCain's absence from the negotiations is hurting efforts to reach an agreement. And activists on both sides of the debate say the change in the senator's profile on the issue is striking. "Why is his name not on it now? Why isn't

he leading the negotiations right now? Because he knows
it's killing him in the primary," Camarota said. "It's an issue
that he could be out front on. He has in the past. He ain't
anymore."[22]

Another report indicated that McCain felt the need to
distance himself from Kennedy; the result was bad news
for the immigration bill.

Most recently, according to aides, McCain objected to a
provision favored by Kennedy that would require guest
workers to receive the prevailing wage for the industry and
region they work in; a similar provision was part of last year's
bill. The delay has frustrated Democrats, several of whom
suggest privately that McCain is concerned about his
standing among conservatives and does not want to again
support a bill with Kennedy, a well-known liberal icon.[23]

When the Senate chose to take up the immigration
legislation again, McCain offered a new amendment that
would appease conservative activists. As the *Hill* reported,
this new amendment's requirement that undocumented
workers pay back taxes would, arguably, cost more to implement than the taxes would bring in.

The back-taxes provision that could trigger the blue slip
came from Sen. John McCain (R-Ariz.), who continues to
take heavy fire on the presidential hustings for supporting
the immigration deal. McCain introduced a back-taxes
amendment after a conference call in which Republican
bloggers mentioned reports that the Bush administration

had asked that this year's bill not force the very costly
process of tax collection among illegal immigrants.[24]

None of this has been lost on Arizona Republicans,
including the precinct chairman in McCain's home district. Rob Haney, in a conversation with me, said he was
offended by McCain's habit of "changing positions on
whatever issues he needs to, to get elected president." He
was particularly peeved about McCain's willingness to "talk
out of both sides of his mouth on the immigration issue."[25]
Haney, a staunch conservative, was amused that McCain
had been able to fool "the liberal media" into reporting
that he is such a straight-talker, "when Arizonans have
known he is just the opposite for years now."

McCain opposed grassroots Republicans like Haney
in 2004 by leading the charge against Proposition 200, a
measure on the Arizona ballot that sought to deny certain public services to undocumented immigrants. Many
Americans would cheer him for this, but for Haney, the issue was McCain's lack of trustworthiness. McCain, he said,
"wouldn't enforce the provisions in the 1986 immigration
bill to protect our borders, and he might claim he will with
this bill, but we know with him what he says and does are
very different."[26] This "lack of integrity or any core principles" is what led Haney and a group of other dedicated
conservatives to draw up resolutions censuring McCain for
being in "dereliction of his duties and responsibilities as a
representative of the citizens of Arizona."[27]

Haney's resolution passed and was offered to the GOP
committee of Maricopa County, the largest in Arizona.

That's when the party establishment, at the behest of McCain, according to Haney, "came after me." McCain's chief of staff visited the Maricopa County Republican's meeting to "warn them against considering the resolution." McCain then put up his own slate of supporters for various positions to overpower Haney and other insurgents. To fund this effort, McCain put together a PAC that received 40 percent of its contributions from San Francisco Democrats Gregory and Lisa Wendt. Bad move. McCain's slate was crushed, even with him on it running for state committeeman. If McCain had just "ignored this effort," Haney told me, and not obsessed over what a district committeeman was doing, "it would have just gone away."

Haney's efforts are only a part of a much broader problem for McCain. The anger is quite palpable among the party's right flank in McCain's home state. The question now is whether a similar disenchantment on the Right will thwart his presidential bid. Given his history, it seems inevitable that reality will clash with the maverick image—at least for those who are paying attention.

TEN

McCain's Cabinet of Horrors

IF, FOR SOME REASON, the American voting public, in all its wisdom, decides to make John McCain this nation's forty-fourth president, one of his first orders of business will be to choose a cabinet to fill out his executive team. Those fifteen posts will be occupied by presidential appointments that are then successfully confirmed by the Senate by a simple majority, which is not always an easy task. At present, the Senate consists of forty-nine members from each of the two major parties, plus two independents—Bernie Sanders of Vermont and Joe Lieberman of Connecticut.

By November, however, this will almost certainly change. With several Republican incumbents—John Sununu of New Hampshire, Susan Collins of Maine, Norm Coleman of Minnesota, and Gordon H. Smith of Oregon—deemed very vulnerable, some people are predicting that the Democrats have a good chance of gaining full control— sixty seats—enough to defeat a filibuster.[1] In addition, several GOP stalwarts are retiring—John Warner of Virginia, Trent Lott of Mississippi, Pete Domenici of New Mexico,

and Wayne Allard of Colorado—and the Democratic Party
is salivating (as am I: *Al Franken Live!* from the Senate chambers, with special guest, the Udall Cousins, Mark and Tom,
aiming for the Allard and Domenici seats, respectively).

If a Democratic majority is in place in January 2009, *its*
first order of business will be to swat away McCain's cabinet
appointments as best it can. Or, in the event that McCain
the Forty-fourth is really the maverick his most ardent ad-
mirers think he is, perhaps there will be some nomina-
tions that the Dems find quite agreeable. Nah.

If I am right about who the Real McCain *really* is, his
choices for cabinet posts, taken in sum, will reflect (1) his
lack of core conservative principles; (2) his desire to
show that he has them; (3) his nasty temper (maybe a few
"middle-finger" choices); (4) his loyalty to Bush war policy; and (5) his mercurial "maverick" nature, which might
at first glance appear evident in a particular choice, but on
closer inspection will reveal itself to be more about some
political expediency or another.

But, since we haven't elected a new president quite yet,
and in furtherance of the enlightenment I have tried to
spread in this tome, I offer a hypothetical McCain cabinet—or at least a partial one. As with the dissection of the
McCain positions on various subjects, a look inside this
cabinet (yes, of horrors) should reveal the heart and soul
of the man, throbbing and smoking. It should scare plenty
of people, as well as enrage them—on both sides of the
aisle. More importantly, it should give the reader pause.
Although it is a one-man/one-vote country, you get, along

with your one elected candidate, many men, and maybe even some women. So, careful what you vote for; you may get a village.

McCain's first choice for his team won't be for a cabinet position per se, but for what is considered a cabinet-level post—the vice-presidential spot. And the Senate won't have anything to say about it. He (it's safe to settle on a gender here) might very well come from the list of cabinet possibilities I lay out below, but in any event, it is the choice that will be made first and no doubt with the ultimate in political calculation to bring out the base—and we know in this context what "base" means. By the way, it's too bad that the gender of the veep choice is so stable—a genius gambit to steal Hillary *or* Obama's thunder in the general election would be to pick Condoleezza Rice as a running mate. The only problem is that conservatives likely would not warm up to a ticket with a black, suspiciously single, pro-choice woman on the ticket. Oh well.

Without further ado, let's get down to the business of assembling Team McCain, with the proviso that what follows is a putative wish list, proposed in the afterglow of victory and in the spirit of making good on promises made in God knows how many back rooms of electoral politicking during the long and circuitous tour of the Straight Talk Express, destination Pennsylvania Avenue.

SECRETARY OF STATE: The first George (I mean Washington) got things rolling pretty well with his first secretary of state, a man by the name of Thomas Jefferson. The post was once a stepping stone to the presidency, as in the case of not only Jefferson, but also Madison, Monroe, Adams, Van Buren, and Buchanan. Then again, the post lent no magic to presidential wannabes such as Ed Muskie or one Walter Q. Gresham (Grover Cleveland's man). Ms. Rice now holds it.

As head of the State Department, the secretary of state is concerned mostly with foreign affairs. Therefore, with the power vested in me, I nominate Paul Wolfowitz as McCain's likely choice for two reasons, one facetious and one real. Facetious going first, I would point out Wolfowitz's demonstrated interest in finding work for his girlfriend who, accustomed to her man's clout at the World Bank, might just find his role at the State Department highly appealing. But seriously speaking, let me remind you that McCain is running on a full commitment to the war in Iraq: Paul Wolfowitz, principal architect. Wolfie at State would go a long way toward making it possible for the war to continue under the man who built it—until the man who built it can finish it. Poetic justice (with tragic undertones).

A second choice, assuming a Wolfowitz appointment gets laughed out of the Senate chambers, would be Richard Armitage, who resigned as undersecretary of state under Colin Powell the day after Powell resigned. Armitage was tough on Musharraf, has a nice mix of the moderate and the hawkish, and might be nominated based on his having a decent chance at being confirmed.

SECRETARY OF THE TREASURY: George Washington made another distinguished appointment, which got Treasury off to a nice start, when he chose Alexander

Hamilton for the post. Although he had his problems with Mr. Jefferson, Hamilton did found the first mint and the first national bank. These days, or shall I say, in times of war and recession, Treasury is a key ally in both fighting and protecting banking. Therefore, Phil Gramm comes to mind. He has a lot going for him: he was once a Democratic Congressman, then he was a Republican Congressman (McCain might like that!) before he became a GOP Senator from Texas. Nowadays, having been passed over for Treasury by Bush, and passed over for the presidency of Texas A&M by a bunch of fellow Texans (dang!), he busies himself as vice president at the investment bank, UBS. (On the side, he is McCain's economic advisor.[2]) Heck, he does have a PhD in economics, is a big friend of banking interests in general, and (seriously folks) is a very likely choice. Professional courtesy to a former senator might make his confirmation actually possible.

SECRETARY OF DEFENSE: Steel yourselves, folks, for a screwball nomination: the shape-changing Joe Lieberman, former Democratic vice-presidential nominee, gets offered the keys to the Pentagon. His appointment is the easiest way for McCain to realize his dream of staying in Iraq. Can the elfin independent be the spokesman for war policy? You just don't know. Both sides of the aisle would like to see him gone, so that confirmation might be by unanimous voice vote. Little Joe has been pro-Iraq war, even if, on social issues, he is not what the base has in mind. The only social line he'd have to hold, however, would be rooting out gays in the military (guys who speak Arabic are creepy enough; gay guys who speak Arabic—nope). But if Joe is a no-go—he may want to stay right where he is, and the McCain people might feel that a woman would make things livelier in the Cabinet meetings—to get coffee and things—the likely-to-be-vanquished Susan Collins of Maine would be a nice recruit. She has been in lockstep with the Bush war plan all along; it didn't do her any good in her home state (hence her likely ouster in November), so she might be rewarded with the job of her life. So it goes.

ATTORNEY GENERAL: This one is delicious and inevitable. Whether there is enough money in it for him is another matter. But my choice as McCain's choice is the one and only . . . America's former Mayor . . . former presumptive Republican presidential nominee . . . and a guy synonymous with standing up to terrorists, at least rhetorically . . . a guy with the lopsided grin of someone who is about to steal your hubcaps . . . Rudolph William Louis Giuliani.

Having ditched the wife and the comb-over, Giuliani took his New York show on the road, went straight to Florida, nipped Ron Paul by a percentage point in the primary, and called it a day.[3] In his time, he has managed to rid New York of squeegee men, antagonize the African American community and, in the aftermath of 9/11, actually anger the decimated brotherhood of New York firefighters, so imagine what damage he could do as America's chief lawyer in control of the Justice Department. Have a scandal in the White House, who you gonna call? And if things went well for him, he might finally be able to find a decent job for his good friend Bernie Kerik.

SECRETARY OF THE INTERIOR: Man, who can possibly replace Dirk Kempthorne! You don't know Dirk? The former governor of and senator from Idaho is renowned for his conservative views, particularly on economic issues. His term as head of the Department of the Interior is notable for two things: he has placed no plants or animals on the federal endangered species list, and, by failing to approve or disapprove a Mohawk casino, he killed it. So he's got the pocket gophers and native Americans against him. He's outta there. I've got just the man to replace him, and it's almost automatic: Conrad Burns from Montana. He's got solid Abramoff connections (sorry, Indians, another bad deal), though this connection was left unexplored by a self-protective McCain when Black Jack was investigated.[4] And Burns is perfect to take care of our Interior, at least in the eyes of the base: in 2005, he got a 5 percent rating from that tree-hugging League of Conservation Voters and a 100 percent rating from the American Land Rights Association. You might wonder what he'd be doing as overseer of the National Park Service if one of the National Park Service's most virulent enemies (the American Land Rights Association) loves him so, but then you'd be naive, wouldn't you. But voters should be wary: since losing his Montana senate seat in 2006, Burns has been very active in his auction business, and he oversees a lot of public land— imagine what Yellowstone would fetch on the open mar-

ket? That American Land Rights Association likes nothing
more than when the government gives the land back to the
people. Then the people can keep other people off it.

SECRETARY OF COMMERCE: This is the one department where there might be a carryover. Why keep Carlos
Gutierrez? I'll tell you why. *Florida.* Gutierrez, born in
Havana, the son of a pineapple plantation owner who was
thrown out of the country during *la revolución,* spent his
childhood in Miami, where he still has roots.[5] Wouldn't
it be nice to win Florida in November? thinks McCain.
Wouldn't it be nice to reassure Mr. Gutierrez that he, as
a Cuban-born secretary of commerce, can stay at his post
in the new post-Fidel era, when the issue of reestablishing
trade with that country heats up? The influential Cuban-
American vote in Florida would be hot to trot for McCain
if they knew that their man from Havana was staying in.
Expect Carlos to continue at Commerce.

SECRETARY OF HOMELAND SECURITY: The Department of Homeland Security (DHS), established in response to 9/11, is only five years old, yet it is the third largest department in the federal government, with 200,000
employees (only Defense and Veteran Affairs are larger).
Everyone knows who the father of Homeland Security is,
but he is abroad and trailing a dialysis machine. At the moment, a former federal judge, Michael Chertoff, runs the
show. He stepped up after Bernie Kerik, citing personal
problems of a legal nature, withdrew his name from con-
sideration as successor to Tom Ridge. It's a tough job running a big department in an administration that doesn't

believe in spending money; perhaps that's why the morale and job satisfaction at DHS is at the bottom of all thirty-six federal agencies.[6] So who's going to agree to run such an agency? If Giuliani doesn't make it as attorney general, Rudy's the choice—the Senate might think his judgement is better in this arena anyway. More likely, this is a job for an ambitious prosecutor, such as Giuilani used to be, such as Michael Chertoff used to be.

Perhaps McCain will dissolve the department—it never existed before Oct. 8, 2001 (as the Office of Homeland Security)—because which politician wants to work this hard? Wait! There has to be a guy with a fence-building company who wants only to get in there to protect us and get a nice contract for his friends in the bargain. Let me find that guy and get back to you. Okay, we're back to Bernie Kerik; I think he knows a fence when he sees one.

SECRETARY OF HEALTH AND HUMAN SERVICES: Is there a doctor in the house? We'll get to that.

Thirty years ago, Jimmy Carter split the Department of Health, Education, and Welfare into two departments, Health and Human Services (HHS) and Education and in the process forever expunged the once-beautiful word "welfare" from official government vocabulary.

Now HHS is concerned solely with your health. And it is time for Bill Frist to come back into public service. This guy is a real doctor as well as a real businessman, and he is worth many millions of dollars because of a family stake in a hospital corporation. Doctors do well; why shouldn't hospitals and hospital corporation stockholders do well, too? Frist served two terms as a Tennessee senator, and, having risen to Senate Majority Leader, declined to run for a third term in 2006. Although he might run for governor in 2010, the limelight could call. And he has the chops of the Republican base: he is pro-life and anti–gay adoption, supports the death penalty, is anti–human cloning, and is decidedly cool to stem cell research. He helped the Republicans out by working hard to defeat Harold Ford in Tennessee last year. The job is his if he wants it, and again, senatorial courtesy would get him confirmed.

SECRETARY OF LABOR: Lots of people would be interested in seeing Ann Coulter in labor, but that's the kind of joke this country doesn't need right now, so I'll quit right there. The labor secretary spot does seem, for some odd reason, to be a job for a woman—only Robert Reich, under Clinton, broke the string of five consecutive female labor secretaries, including the current one, Elaine Chao. There have been six female labor chiefs all told—more than for any other department—going back to Frances Perkins, the first woman cabinet member ever and FDA's labor secretary for twelve years. During her tenure she oversaw the New Deal and the founding of the minimum wage law and the Social Security administration. This was some woman! And so is the last surviving member of the original Bush cabinet, Elaine Chao, who is to organized labor what George W. Bush is to diction. She's seen in many quarters as a sell-out to big business (see, for example, www.shameonelaine.org).[7] But heck, she's Kentucky Senator Mitch McConnell's wife, she's well connected, and something tells me that, if we end up with McCain the Forty-fourth, Elaine Chao's fate might be to serve as long as Frances Perkins—but she's no Frances Perkins.

All that said, your guesses are as good as mine. Would Mitt "there are cars in my blood" Romney accept the Transportation post or does he feel he needs to recoup the $36 million he lost on his run for the White House?[8] Can George Allen be renovated as secretary of Housing and Urban Development? (He'd be a real fixer-upper, but anything's possible.) Personally, I look forward to the sanctimonious Rick Santorum getting over his snit with McCain—especially if he's offered a post, like Education, in which he could push an atavistic agenda and get vouchers through for the sake of parochial school redoubts for white folk.

Agriculture: give me some King Corn from a big Corn State, I don't care who. But you know, sure as shooting, that a staple of every Republican energy policy is a mug of oil and a side of corn. So Agriculture better be sweet on Energy, which will go to a man from a state with plenty of drilling—you might say Don Nichols from Oklahoma or John Breaux from Louisiana. (Breaux is a Democrat but steeped in offshore crude.)

Lastly, though, I have a wish . . . a prediction wrapped up in a wish. It is this: if, indeed, there is the slightest maverick lurking inside John Sidney McCain III, he will make a statement to the Swift Boaters and the nastier elements of the party he calls his own and offer the post at Veterans Affairs to Max Cleland. Cleland, a Democrat and a disabled

Vietnam vet, lost his Georgia Senate seat, in large part owing to TV ads pairing Cleland with Osama bin Laden and implying that Cleland was soft on homeland security. McCain denounced the ads, which were discontinued, but it was too late for Cleland, who lost to Saxby Chambliss.

But the John McCain who denounced those ads was an older version of the man, not McCain 3.0, the man who would be president, circa 2008. Perhaps McCain is the only one who thinks he is steadfast in his beliefs, the McCain who hoped to live up to the late Senator Goldwater, who was the man with a reputation for straight talk wider than the Grand Canyon.

But that McCain no longer is with us, if he ever truly was. Barry's strikingly similar–looking nephew Don—a losing candidate for the Republican nomination for governor of Arizona in 2006—summed it up when we met at the Maricopa Republican Party headquarters in June 2007. Slowly shaking his head in disgust, he said, "I knew Barry Goldwater, and John McCain is no Barry Goldwater."[9] Nor is he a maverick, independent, or reformer, as this book has made, I hope, abundantly clear.

Notes

CHAPTER ONE

1. John McCain, interview by Miles O'Brien, *American Morning with Miles O'Brien*, CNN, February 23, 2007.

2. National Religious Broadcasters, "Who We Are—Statement of Faith and Code of Ethics," www.nrb.org/CC_Content_Page/0,,PTID3 08766|CHID568980,00.html.

3. Brendan Farrington, "McCain Defends Christian Outreach Effort," Associated Press, February 17, 2007, www.abcnews.com.

4. Ibid.

5. The Club for Growth, "John McCain's Record on Economic Issues," March 12, 2007, www.clubforgrowth.org/2007/03/arizona _senator_john_mccains_t.php.

6. Jacob Weisberg, "The Closet McCain: Psst . . . He's Not Really a Conservative," *Slate*, April 12, 2006, www.slate.com/id/2139775.

7. Michael Gaynor, "The Case for Mitt: Economy, Judges," January 24, 2008, www.theconservativevoice.com.

8. Shawn Zeller, "McCain POW Record Attacked, Again," *St. Petersburg Times*, January 17, 2008, www.politifact.com/truth-o-meter/article/ 2008/jan/17/mccains-pow-record-attacked.

9. Dan Nowicki and Bill Muller, "Arizona, the Early Years," *Arizona Republic*, March 1, 2007.

10. Steve Benen, "High Infidelity: What If Three Admitted Adulterers Run for President and No One Cares," *Washington Monthly*,

July/August 2006, www.washingtonmonthly.com/features/2006/0607. benen.html.

11. Greg Boguslavsky, "The Dartmouth Review Interview: John McCain," *Dartmouth Review,* December 8, 2007.

12. John Judis, "Neo-McCain: The Making of an Uberhawk," *New Republic,* October 16, 2006.

13. Sandra Wittman, "Chronology of U.S.–Vietnam Relations," *Vietnam: Yesterday and Today,* www.oakton.edu/user/~wittman/ chronol.htm.

14. Mark R. Levin, "Remember the Keating Five?" *National Review Online,* April 5, 2001.

15. Ibid.

16. Ibid.

17. *Bipartisan Campaign Reform Act,* Public Law 107–155, 107th Congress (March 27, 2002), 116 stat. 81.

18. "Media Matters for America Summary," October 30, 2006, www.mediamatters.com; Richard H. Davis, "The Anatomy of a Smear Campaign," *Boston Globe,* March 21, 2004.

19. Maureen Dowd, "Liberties: High and Low," *New York Times,* December 3, 2000.

20. Cliff Schecter, "Extremely Motivated: The Republican Party's March to the Right," *Fordham Urban Law Journal* 29, no. 4 (April 2002).

21. CNN, "McCain Denies Party Witch and Presidential Run," June 2, 2001, *CNN.com.*

22. Glen Johnson, "For Kerry Aides, McCain Would Fit Bill as Running Mate," *Boston Globe,* April 6, 2004.

23. Terry Neal, "McCain Softens Abortion Stand," *Washington Post,* August 24, 1999.

CHAPTER TWO

1. David Greenberg, "Goldwater's Glitter," *The American Prospect,* June 1996.

2. Dan Nowicki and Bill Muller, "McCain Becomes the Maverick," *Arizona Republic*, March 1, 2007.

3. Ibid.

4. John McCain, interviewed by Chris Matthews, *Hardball*, MSNBC, September 10, 2006.

5. Ryan Lizza, "On the Bus," *New Yorker*, February 25, 2008, 30.

6. Paul Kane, "Capitol Briefing," *Washington Post*, April 26, 2007.

7. United States Senate, "U.S. Senate Roll Call Votes 110th Congress—1st Session," www.senate.gov/legislative/LIS/roll_call _lists/roll_call_vote_cfm.cfm?congress=110&session=1&vote=00073.

8. Think Progress, "McCain Skips Petraeus Briefing to Campaign in New Hampshire," April 25, 2007, http://thinkprogress.org/2007/ 04/25/mccain-petraeus.

9. KCPW, "Arizona Senator John McCain Speaks at the Utah State Republican Convention," 1010 AM, Salt Lake City, Utah, May 13, 2006, www.kcpw.org/article/658.

10. Ibid.

11. Sam Youngman, "McCain's Missed Votes on Iraq Triggers Reid Rebuke," *The Hill*, May 17, 2007, http://thehill.com/leading-the-news/ mccains-missed-votes-on-iraq-trigger-reid-rebuke-2007-05-17.html.

12. United Steelworkers (USW), "Ted Kennedy Blasts Senate Republicans over Minimum Wage," January 25, 2007, www.usw.org/ usw/program/content/3725.php.

13. Think Progress, "McCain Rated as America's Worst Senator for Children," February 27, 2008, http://thinkprogress.org/2008/02/27/ mccain-children.

14. The 2007 Children's Defense Fund Action Council Non-partisan Congressional Scorecard, "Did Your Members of Congress Protect Children?" February 2008, www.childrensdefense.org/site/ DocServer/2007_Scorecard.pdf?docID=6401.

15. Dana Priest and Anne Hull, "Soldiers Face Neglect, Frustration at Army's Top Medical Facility," *Washington Post*, February 18, 2007, A01.

16. Jim Webb, U.S. Senator for Virginia, "Senator Jim Webb's Opening Remarks Regarding His G.I. Education Legislation before Committee on Veterans' Affairs," press release, May 9, 2007, http://webb.senate.gov/newsroom/record.cfm?id=273786.

17. David Ignatius, "A Man Who Won't Sell His Soul," *Washington Post*, May 3, 2006, A23.

CHAPTER THREE

1. Joel Connelly and Ed Offley, "McCain and Bush Clash over Revs. Robertson, Falwell," *Seattle Post-Intelligencer*, February 29, 2000.

2. Ari Berman, "The Real McCain," *The Nation*, December 12, 2005.

3. Jerry Falwell, "1999 fund-raising letter," *Church & State*, October 1999, 9.

4. Cliff Schecter, "Extremely Motivated: The Republican Party's March to the Right," *Fordham Urban Law Journal* 29, no. 4 (April 2002).

5. Ibid.

6. John McCain, interview by Amy Goodman, *Democracy Now*, September 3, 2004.

7. Michael Roston, "Anti-McCain Vets Ready Salvo against Senator's Presidential Campaign," *Raw Story*, March 9, 2007, http://rawstory.com/news/2007/AntiMcCain_vets_ready_their_salvo_against_0302.html.

8. Chris Suellentrop, "For Shame: A Leaked Video Reveals What Bob Dole Really Thinks about Bush's Tactics," *Slate*, August 27, 2004.

9. Robert Philpot, "Senator Double Talk: John McCain, Star Turn at the Tory Conference Last Night, Is Not All He Seems," Comment is Free . . . Blog, *Guardian Unlimited* (UK), October 2, 2006, http://commentisfree.guardian.co.uk/robert_philpot/2006/10/the_tories_mr_double_talk.html.

10. Media Matters for America, "Who Is McCain Campaign Manager Terry Nelson? And Will the Media Tell Us?" December 14, 2006, http://mediamatters.org/items/200612140001.

11. America Votes, "Political Drama Unfolds as Letter Carriers Fail to Deliver: Kerry, Bush Camps Weigh in on Ad Controversy," *CNN.com*, August 26, 2004, www.cnn.com/2004/ALLPOLITICS/08/25/cleland. swiftboat/index.html.

12. CBS News, "McCain's Letter to Obama: Text of Republican Senator's Letter on Lobbying Reform," February 7, 2006, www.cbsnews .com/stories/2006/02/07/politics/main1289745.shtml.

13. John McCain, interview by Chris Matthews, "McCain vs. Obama on Lobbying Reform," *Hardball*, MSNBC, February 8, 2006, www.msnbc.msn.com/id/11221077.

14. Political Radar Blog, "McCain: Why Can't We Be Friends," ABC News, January 9, 2008, http://blogs.abcnews.com/politicalradar/ 2008/01/mccain-why-cant.html.

15. Sidney Blumenthal, "The Fighting Side of McCain," *Salon.com*, January 18, 2007, www.salon.com/opinion/blumenthal/2007/01/18/ mccain.

16. Paul Kane, "McCain, Cornyn Engage in Heated Exchange," Capitol Briefing Blog, *Washington Post*, http://blog.washingtonpost. com/capitol-briefing/2007/05/mccain_cornyn_cursing_showdown .html.

17. Ralph Vartabedian and Michael Finnegan, "Legendary Temper Could Undermine McCain," *Los Angeles Times*, May 25, 2007.

18. Ronald Kessler, "McCain's Out-of-Control Anger: Does He Have the Temperament to Be President?" *Newsmax*, July 5, 2006, http://archive.newsmax.com/archives/articles/2006/7/5/00548 .shtml.

19. Libby Quaid, "McCain's Sharp Tongue: An Achilles Heel?" *Huffington Post*, February 16, 2008, www.huffingtonpost.com/2008/ 02/16/mccains-sharp-tongue-an_n_87012.html.

20. Harry Jaffe, "Senator Hothead," *Washingtonian*, February 1997.

21. Tim Russert, interview by Joe Scarborough, *Morning Joe*, MSNBC, February 6, 2008.

CHAPTER FOUR

1. George Washington, "Farewell Address, 1796," Avalon Project at Yale Law School, www.yale.edu/lawweb/avalon/washing.htm.

2. John McCain, "Rogue State Rollback," *The Weekly Standard* 8, no. 18 (January 20, 2003).

3. Matt Welch, "Senator Mc-Cut-and-Run," *Los Angeles Times,* January 16, 2007, http://opinion.latimes.com/opinionla/2007/01/senator_mccutan.html.

4. John McCain, interview by Tim Russett, *Meet the Press,* NBC, May 13, 2008.

5. CNN, "Bin Laden, Millionaire with a Dangerous Grudge," September 27, 2001, www.cnn.com/2001/US/09/12/binladen.profile/index.html.

6. C-SPAN2, John McCain speech, October 6, 1994.

7. John Judis, "Neo-McCain: The Making of an Uberhawk," *New Republic,* October 16, 2006.

8. Rachel Landau, "United States Military Actions since Vietnam," Associated Press, March 24, 1999, *Boston Globe,* http://boston.com/news/packages/kosovo/pastengagements.htm; John Judis, "Neo-McCain: The Making of an Uberhawk," *New Republic,* October 16, 2006.

9. Vin Weber, "Bosnia: Strange Alliances," *National Review Online,* June 7, 1993.

10. "Q&A with John McCain: Why Senate Skeptic Backed Bosnia Mission," *International Herald Tribune,* January 8, 1996.

11. Paul Hackett, interview by author, April 14, 2007.

12. Sasha Issenberg, "Political Realist Now Follows His Own Path," *Boston Globe,* November, 23, 2007.

13. John Judis, "Neo-McCain: The Making of an Uberhawk," *New Republic,* October 16, 2006.

14. Ibid.

15. Project for the New American Century, Letter to President

Clinton, January 26, 1998, www.newamericancentury.org/iraq
clintonletter.htm.

CHAPTER FIVE

1. John McCain, "Rogue State Rollback," *The Weekly Standard,*
January 20, 2003.

2. Shadia B. Drury, *Leo Strauss and the American Right,* (New York:
St. Martin's Press, 1999).

3. Political Research Associates, "Randy Scheunemann, Profile,"
publiceye.org, October 5, 2007, http://rightweb.irc-online.org/
profile/1347.

4. Paul Rieckhoff, interview by author, March 2007.

5. Larry Johnson, interview by author, April 2007.

6. Joe Klein, "Talking Heads," Swampland Blog, *Time.com,* February
4, 2007, http://time-blog.com/swampland/2007/02/talking_heads
.html.

7. Greg Sargent, "Joe Klein: McCain's Been " 'Entirely Consistent'
On Iraq War," Horse's Mouth Blog, *TalkingPointsMemo.com,* February 5,
2007, www.talkingpointsmemo.com/horsesmouth/2007/02/joe_klein
_mccai.php.

8. Ibid.

9. Gloria Borger, "Does Barack Really Rock?" *U.S. News & World
Report,* October 29, 2006, http://www.usnews.com/usnews/news/
articles/061029/6glo_2.htm.

10. David Brock and Paul Waldman, *Free Ride: John McCain and the
Media* (Anchor Books: New York, 2008).

11. Think Progress, "McCain Claims He Knew Iraq War Would Be
'Long and Hard and Tough,' Contradicting Pre-War Statements," January 4, 2007, http://thinkprogress.org/2007/01/04/mccain-iraq-easy.

12. Ibid.

13. Glenn Greenwald, "John McCain Unveils His Grand Plan for
Victory in Iraq," Unclaimed Territory, October 20, 2006, http://

glenngreenwald.blogspot.com/2006/10/john-mccain-unveils-his
-grand-plan-for.html.

14. Ibid.

15. Think Progress, "Hagel: McCain Resolution Is 'Disingenuous'
and 'Intellectually Dishonest,'" February 4, 2007, http://thinkprogress
.org/2007/02/04/hagel-mccain.

16. Judy Mathewson, "Brzezinski Calls Idea to Boost U.S. Forces in
Iraq a 'Gimmick,'" November 24, 2006, www.bloomberg.com/apps/
news?pid=20601070&refer=home&sid=aReG3cWAXnFA.

17. John Judis, "Neo-McCain: The Making of an Uberhawk," *New
Republic,* October 16, 2006.

18. John McCain, interview by Wolf Blitzer, *Late Edition,* CNN,
September 9, 2002.

19. John McCain, interview by George Stephanopoulos, *This Week,*
ABC, October 24, 2004, http://biden.senate.gov/newsroom/details.
cfm?id=227713&&.

20. John McCain, interview on *CBS Early Show,* June 29, 2005,
http://www.youtube.com/watch?v=h9OGGI8aAwE&feature
=related.

21. Byron York, "America's (Second) Most Important Hawk,"
The Hill, December 8, 2005, http://thehill.com/byron-york/
americas-second-most-important-hawk-2005-12-08.html.

22. Andrew Clevenger, "McCain Stumps for Wakim at City
Luncheon," *Charleston Gazette,* October 17, 2006.

23. Roger Simon, "McCain Bashes Cheney over Iraq Policy,"
Politico, January 24, 2007, http://www.politico.com/news/stories/
0107/2390.html.

24. John McCain, interview by Anderson Cooper, Anderson
Cooper Blog 360°, January 29, 2007, www.cnn.com/CNN/Programs/
anderson.cooper.360/blog/2007/01/mccain-clinton-obama-iraq
-plans-lack.html.

25. Bethany Thomas, "McCain to Focus on Electability," MSNBC

.com, January 24, 2008, http://firstread.msnbc.msn.com/archive/ 2008/01/24/606802.aspx.

26. Think Progress, "McCain Flip-Flops in 47 Seconds: Claims Success Is Not Realistic in 'A Few Months,' Then Says It Is," from ABC, April 4, 2007, http://thinkprogress.org/2007/02/04/mccain-flip.

27. Think Progress, "Americans Don't Trust McCain's View on Iraq," April 11, 2007, http://thinkprogress.org/2007/04/11/ americans-dont-trust-mccains-view-on-iraq.

28. Think Progress, "McCain: 'I Know What's Best for the Security of This Nation,'" April 17, 2007, http://thinkprogress.org/2007/04/ 17/mccain-knows-best.

29. Think Progress, "Faced with Facts, McCain Denies His Own Straight Talk," March 28, 2007, http://thinkprogress.org/2007/03/ 28/roberts-cnn-mccain-iraq.

30. AFP, "McCain Defends Baghdad Market Stroll," *Raw Story,* April 8, 2007, http://rawstory.com/news/afp/McCain_defends _Baghdad_market_strol_04082007.html.

31. Kirk Semple, "McCain Wrong on Iraq Security, Merchants Say," *New York Times,* April 3, 2007.

32. *Think Progress,* "CNN: Military Sources Respond to McCain's Escalation Remark with 'Laughter Down the Line,'" March 27, 2007, http://thinkprogress.org/2007/03/27/ware-mccain-iraq.

33. Larry Johnson, interview by author, April 2007.

34. Matt Taibbi, "Giuliani: Worse Than Bush," *Rolling Stone,* June 14, 2007, www.rollingstone.com/politics/story/14952564/giuliani_ worse_than_bush/3.

35. Arianna Huffington, "Davos Notes: John McCain Bites My Head Off," *Huffington Post,* January 27, 2007, www.huffingtonpost .com/arianna-huffington/davos-notes-john-mccain-_b_39788.html.

36. ABC News, "John McCain to Murtha: 'Lighten Up,' 'Get a Life,'" *ABCNews.com,* April 26, 2007, http://abcnews.go.com/GMA/ story?id=3082244.

37. John McCain, interview by Tim Russert, *Meet the Press*, MSNBC, January 21, 2007.

38. "Sen. John McCain Delivers Remarks on Iraq," *Washington Post*, April 11, 2007, http://www.washingtonpost.com/wp-dyn/content/article/2007/04/11/AR2007041101074.html.

39. Think Progress, "Webb: McCain Is Consistently 'Impugning People's Patriotism' and 'Hiding behind the Troops,'" April 14, 2007, http://thinkprogress.org/2007/04/14/webb-mccain.

40. TPMCafe.com, April 11, 2007, http://electioncentral.tpmcafe.com/blog/electioncentral/2007/apr/11/mccain_video.

41. Think Progress, "After Blaming Clinton for North Korea Nuke, McCain Blasts People 'Engaging in Finger-Pointing,'" October 11, 2006, http://thinkprogress.org/2006/10/11/mccain-nk.

42. David Edwards and Ron Brynaert, "Unplugged McCain Sings 'Bomb bomb bomb, bomb bomb Iran,'" Raw Story, April 19, 2007, http://rawstory.com/news/2007/McCain_unplugged_Bomb_bomb_bomb_bomb_0419.html.

43. Associated Press, "Giuliani, McCain: U.S. Should Prepare to Use Force against Iran," October 16, 2007, http://www.haaretz.com/hasen/spages/913507.html.

44. Steven Kull, "What Kind of Foreign Policy Does the American Public Want?" PIPA/Knowledge Networks Poll, October 20, 2006, http://www.worldpublicopinion.org/pipa/pdf/oct06/SecurityFP_Oct06_rpt.pdf.

CHAPTER SIX

1. John Solomon, "One Time Reformer Taps Big Donors," *Washington Post*, February 11, 2007.

2. Chris Suellentrop, "Is John McCain a Crook?" *Slate.com*, February 18, 2000, www.slate.com/id/1004633.

3. Walter V. Robinson, "Pluck, Leaks, Helped McCain to Overcome S&L Scandal," *Boston Globe*, February 29, 2000.

4. Bill Muller and Dan Nowicki, "The Keating Five," *Arizona Republic*, March 1, 2007, www.azcentral.com/news/specials/mccain/articles/0301mccainbio-chapter7.html.

5. Robinson, "Pluck, Leaks, Helped McCain to Overcome S&L Scandal"; Suellentrop, "Is John McCain a Crook?"

6. Richard L. Berke, "An Angry DeConcini Defends His Ethics," *New York Times*, November 20, 1990.

7. Public Citizen, "Introduction to Bipartisan Campaign Reform Act of 2002 (BCRA)," http://www.citizen.org/congress/campaign/legislation/bcralaw/articles.cfm?ID=15196.

8. *Congressional Record*, Senate Vote 9, S 2: Congressional Compliance—Personal Use of Campaign Funds, January 10, 1995 (Motion agreed to 64-35: R 52-1; D 12-34).

9. *Congressional Record*, U.S. Senate Roll Call Votes 104th Congress, 1st Session, "To maintain public funding for Presidential campaigns"; S. Amdt. 1153, http://thomas.loc.gov/cgi-bin/bdquery/z?d104:SP1153:; S. Con. Res. 13, http://thomas.loc.gov/cgi-bin/bdquery/z?d104:SC00013:; McCain's No Vote, http://www.senate.gov/legislative/LIS/roll_call_lists/roll_call_vote_cfm.cfm?congress=104&session=1&vote=00194.

10. Campaign for Responsive Politics, "McCain Tapping Smaller Donors in Presidential Money Race," *Washington Post*, February 17, 2000, http://www.opensecrets.org/pressreleases/feb17_00_release.htm.

11. George Will, "McCain Shows Disturbing Righteousness," *Detroit News*, March 2, 2008.

12. Michael D. Shear and Jeffrey H. Birnbaum, "The Anti-Lobbyist, Advised by Lobbyists," *Washington Post*, February 22, 2008.

13. Josh Gerstein, "Campaign Finance Effort Resumes, without McCain," *New York Sun*, July 28, 2006.

14. Editorial, "A Retreat toward Watergate," *New York Times*, August 18, 2006, www.nytimes.com/2006/08/18/opinion/18fri2.html?_r=2&oref=slogin&pagewanted=print.

15. John McCain, interview with Terry Moran, Straight Talk Express in Grafton, New Hampshire, March 24, 2007.

16. Bob Bauer, "McCain and His Law," *New York Sun*, March 8, 2007.

17. Anne E. Kornblut and Walter V. Robinson, "McCain Interceded for Donors, Data Show," *Boston Globe*, January 9, 2000.

18. Ibid.

19. Allpolitics.com, "Industries Help Fund McCain PAC," *CNN.com*, July 19, 2000, http://archives.cnn.com/2000/ALLPOLITICS/stories/07/19/mccain.fundraising.ap/index.html.

20. McCain Mutiny, "Paxson Contradicts McCain," February 23, 2008, http://themccainmutiny.com/2008/02/23/paxson-contradicts-mccain.

21. Media Matters, "Brewer and Stoddard Failed to Note FCC Chairman's Criticism of McCain's Letter for Paxson," February 22, 2008, http://mediamatters.org/items/200802220005.

22. Capital Eye, "Jack Abramoff Lobbying and Political Contributions, 1999–2006," January 12, 2006, http://www.capitaleye.org/abramoff_recips.asp.

23. James V. Grimaldi, "Probe of Abramoff and Nonprofits' Money Opens," *Washington Post*, March 17, 2005, www.washingtonpost.com/wp-dyn/articles/A41850-2005Mar16.html.

24. Alexander Bolton, "Eyeing '08, Sen. McCain Courts K St.," *The Hill*, March 8, 2006, http://thehill.com/leading-the-news/eyeing—08-sen.-mccain-courts-k-st.-2006-03-08.html.

CHAPTER SEVEN

1. Greg Giroux, "McCain's Campaign: Major Donors," *New York Times*, February 1, 2007, www.nytimes.com/cq/2007/02/01/cq_2221.html.

2. Jim Rassmann, "Shame on the Swift Boat Veterans for Bush," *Wall Street Journal*, August 10, 2004.

3. Jill Lawrence, "McCain Sick and Tired of Re-fighting Vietnam War," *USA Today*, August 25, 2004, www.usatoday.com/news/politics elections/nation/president/2004-08-25-mccain-_x.htm.

4. Federal Election Commission, "Swift Boat Vets and POWs for Truth," Disclosure Report, http://query.nictusa.com/cgi-bin/com _ind/C00431734.

5. This figure reflects data from the *Congressional Quarterly*'s PoliticalMoneyLine and includes only donations from individuals or married couples directly to John McCain or his PAC, Straight Talk America. It does not include contributions from other PACs the Swifties support that gave money to McCain or his committee.

6. Political Campaign $$$ Contributors by Last Name, http:// campaignmoney.com.

7. Associated Press, "John Kerry Accepts Boone Pickens' Swift Boat Challenge," *Dallas News*, November 16, 2007.

8. Todd Purdum, "Prisoner of Conscience," *Vanity Fair*, February 2007, www.vanityfair.com/politics/features/2007/02/mccain200702.

9. Patrick O'Conner, "Renzi Paid over $100,000 in Legal Fees This Year," *Politico*, April 12, 2007, www.politico.com/blogs/thecrypt/0407/ Renzi_Paid_Over_100000_In_Legal_Fees_This_Year.html.

10. Matt Ortega, "McCain Praised Renzi's Honesty and Integrity in 2006 Robo-Call," Democratic Party Blog, February 22, 2008, www .democrats.org/a/2008/02/trying_to_get_a.php.

11. FEC, 2004.

12. David Johnston, "The 2006 Campaign: Congressman from Arizona Is the Focus of an Inquiry," *New York Times*, October 25, 2006, http://select.nytimes.com/2006/10/25/washington/25inquire .html?_r=1.

13. Alexander Bolton, "Renzi Didn't Reveal $200K," *The Hill*, April 25, 2007, http://thehill.com/leading-the-news/renzi-didnt-reveal -200k-2007-04-25.html.

14. Ibid.

15. Paul Kiel, "Breaking: GOP Rep Renzi Indicted," *TPM Muck-*

raker, February 22, 2008, http://tpmmuckraker.talkingpointsmemo
.com/2008/02/breaking_gop_rep_renzi_indicte.php.

16. Think Progress, "McCain Witholds 'Judgment' on Renzi
Indictment," February 22, 2008, http://thinkprogress.org/2008/
02/22/mccain-witholds-judgment-on-renzi-indictment.

17. *Washington Post*, "Renzi Aide's Call to U.S. Attorney Inflames
Dems," April 26, 2007, www.azcentral.com/arizonarepublic/news/
articles/0426probes-renzi0426.html.

18. Lara Lakes Jordan, "Congressman Charged in Land Deal,"
Associated Press, February 23, 2008, http://rawstory.com/news/
mochila/Congressman_charged_in_land_deal_02222008.html.

19. Chris Cillizza, "McCain Continues to Win Over Bush Insiders,"
The Fix, *Washington Post*, http://blog.washingtonpost.com/thefix/
2006/12/mccain_moves_forward.html.

20. Christopher Sherman, "State Rep. Bob Allen Insists He's
Innocent, Will Not Quit," *Orlando Sentinel*, July 13, 2007.

21. Emil Steiner, "Elected Official Blames His Arrest on Fear of
Black People," OFF/beat Blog, *Washington Post*, August 7, 2007,
http://blog.washingtonpost.com/offbeat/2007/08/fl_rep_bob_
allen_blames_his_ar_1.html.

22. Arizona Congress Watch, "Hayworth Used $200K in Campaign
Funds for Legal Fees," July 16, 2007, http://www.azcongresswatch
.com/?cat=13.

23. Jonathan Riskind, "Ex-Aide Calls Ney Advocate for Abramoff,"
Columbus Dispatch, May 31, 2006, http://www.columbusdispatch.com/
live/contentbe/EPIC_shim.php?story=189328.

24. Cliff Schecter, "Sweetheart Deal," *Salon.com*, October 5, 2004,
http://dir.salon.com/story/news/feature/2004/10/05/lobbyist/
index.html?pn=2.

25. Ibid.

26. Billy House, "McCain under Fire for Fundraiser," *Arizona
Republic*, October 6, 2006.

27. Dave McKenna, "Public Noose-ance," City Desk Blogs,

Washington City Paper, January 25, 2008, www.washingtoncitypaper. com/blogs/citydesk/2008/01/25/public-noose-ance.

28. Jonathan Singer, "AP: George Allen in Ethics Heat," MyDD, October 8, 2006, www.mydd.com/story/2006/10/8/14022/3817.

CHAPTER EIGHT

1. Ari Berman, "So Much for Straight Talk," *The Nation,* March 28, 2006, www.thenation.com/blogs/notion?bid=15&pid=72591.

2. The 700 Club, "Interview with Jerry Falwell," *CBN,* September 13, 2001, http://www.actupny.org/YELL/falwell.html.

3. Debra Nussbaum Cohen, "Falwell Antichrist Remark Sparks Anti-Semitism Charges," *Jewish News Weekly,* January 22, 1999.

4. BBC News, "Gay Tinky Winky Bad for Children," February 15, 1999, http://news.bbc.co.uk/2/hi/entertainment/276677.stm.

5. Amy Shatz, "Republicans Mourn Falwell," Washington Wire, *Wall Street Journal,* May 15, 2007, http://blogs.wsj.com/washwire/2007/05/15/republicans-mourn-falwell.

6. Political Ticker, "McCain Says He Hopes to Make Amends with Dobson," *CNN.com,* January 16, 2007, www.cnn.com/POLITICS/blogs/politicalticker/2007/01/mccain-says-he-hopes-to-make-amends.html.

7. Maya Bell, "Sophisticated Tactics Aid Schiavo's Parents," *Bradenton Herald,* March 14, 2005, http://www.bradenton.com.mld/bradenton/news/local/11129371.htm.

8. Reverend Richard Land, interview by Chris Wallace, *Fox News Sunday,* Fox News Channel, May 5, 2007.

9. Ibid.

10. Wayne Slater, "In Dallas, McCain Says He's Reached Out to Many Evangelicals," *Dallas Morning News,* February 6, 2007, www .dallasnews.com/sharedcontent/dws/news/politics/national/stories/DN-mccain_06nat.ART.State.Edition1.295b34f.html.

11. Max Blumenthal, "Birth Pangs of a New Christian Zionism,"

The Nation, August 8, 2006, www.thenation.com/doc/20060814/new_christian_zionism; see also Sarah Posner, *God's Profits: Faith, Fraud, and the Republican Crusade for Values Voters* (Sausalito, CA: PoliPointPress, 2008).

12. Off the Bus, "John Hagee's McCain Endorsement Sparks Uproar," *Huffington Post,* February 29, 2008, www.huffingtonpost.com/2008/02/29/john-hagees-mccain-endor_n_89189.html.

13. Bob Fitrakis, "Theocracy Rising: Blackwell and Parsley Intend to Hijack Ohio," *Free Press,* October 27, 2005, www.freepress.org/departments/display/18/2005/1533.

14. John McCain, interview by Jon Stewart, *Daily Show,* Comedy Central, April 4, 2006.

15. Ibid.

16. John McCain, interview by Larry King, *Larry King Live,* CNN, November 3, 2005, http://transcripts.cnn.com/TRANSCRIPTS/0511/03/lkl.01.html.

17. Joseph Farah, "Christian McCainiacs," *WorldNetDaily.com,* February 12, 2007, www.worldnetdaily.com/news/article.asp?Article_ID=54207.

18. Carla Marinucci, "McCain Gets Boost from Bush's Troubles," *San Francisco Chronicle,* August 20, 1999, http://www.sfgate.com/cgi-bin/article.cgi?f=/c/a/1999/08/20/MN75761.DTL&hw=Roe+Wade&sn=001&sc=1000.

19. Terry M. Neal, "McCain Softens Abortion Stand," *Washington Post,* August 24, 1999, www.washingtonpost.com/wp-srv/politics/campaigns/wh2000/stories/mccain082499.htm.

20. John McCain, interviewed by George Stephanopoulos, ABC's *This Week,* November 19, 2006.

21. John McCain, interview by Tim Russert, *Meet the Press,* MSNBC, May 12, 2007.

22. Media Matters, "Blitzer Ignored McCain's Inconsistencies on Issues, Gave Short Shrift to Other '08 Hopefuls," November 17, 2006, http://mediamatters.org/items/200611180003.

23. "The Imperial Presidency 2.0," *New York Times*, editorial page, January 7, 2007, www.nytimes.com/2007/01/07/opinion/07sun1.html.

24. Carie Budoff, "Anybody but McCain, Santorum Says," *Politico*, March 1, 2007, http://www.politico.com/news/stories/0307/2963.html.

25. Joe Gigante, interview by author, March 2007.

26. On the Issues, "John McCain on VoteMatch," www.massscorecard.org/John_McCain_VoteMatch.htm.

27. Adam Nagourney, "McCain Stumbles on H.I.V. Prevention," The Caucus, *New York Times*, March 16, 2007, http://thecaucus.blogs.nytimes.com/2007/03/16/mccain-stumbles-on-hiv-prevention.

28. Steve Benen, "Why John McCain Will Never Win the Republican Presidential Nomination," *Carpetbagger Report*, March 17, 2007, www.thecarpetbaggerreport.com/archives/10239.html.

29. Matt Welch, "Be Afraid of President McCain," *Reason Online*, April 2007, www.reason.com/news/show/118937.html.

30. Scott Swenson, "Burying Release of Abstinence Only Report on Friday the 13th Seems Fitting," RH Blog, April 13, 2007, www.rhrealitycheck.org/blog/2007/04/13/burying-release-of-abstinence-only-report-on-friday-the-13th-seems-fitting.

31. Jim Davenport, "McCain to Preach Abstinence in S.C.," *SFGate.com*, February 16, 2007, www.sfgate.com/cgi-bin/article.cgi?file=/n/a/2007/02/16/politics/p144216S42.DTL.

32. Nicholas, D. Kristof, "P.O.W. to Power Broker, a Chapter Most Telling," *New York Times*, February 27, 2000, http://query.nytimes.com/gst/fullpage.html?res=9B02EFDF1439F934A15751C0A9669C8B63.

33. Steve Benen, "High Infidelity: What If Three Admitted Adulterers Run for President and No One Cares," *Washington Monthly*, July/August 2006, www.washingtonmonthly.com/features/2006/0607.benen.html.

34. Mike Baker, "McCain: Keep 2008 Spotlight off Gossip," *Washington Post*, March 9, 2007, http://www.washingtonpost.com/wp-dyn/content/article/2007/03/09/AR2007030901416.html.

35. Transcript of John McCain's roundtable discussion with *Arizona Star* editors, *Arizona Star*, August 28, 2005, www.azstarnet.com/sn/opinion/90521.

36. John Shovelan, "Maverick McCain Tones Down on the Polemics," ABC, April 3, 2006, http://www.abc.net.au/worldtoday/content/2006/s1607432.htm.

37. *The Hotline*, "McCain and Creationism: Not In Science Class, but Let Localities Decide," May 9, 2007, http://hotlineblog.national journal.com/archives/2007/05/mccain_and_crea.html.

38. Jacob Weisberg, "The Closet McCain: Psst . . . He's Not Really a Conservative," *Slate*, April 12, 2006, www.slate.com/id/2139775.

39. Russell Berman, "Log Cabin Group Lists Giuliani as Ideal Republican," *New York Sun*, March 23, 2007, www.nysun.com/article/51010.

40. John Aravosis, "John McCain: I Think Gay Marriage Should Be Allowed, but Not Legal," Americablog, October 19, 2006, www.americablog.com/2006/10/john-mccain-i-think-gay-marriage.html.

41. John McCain, interviewed by George Stephanopoulos, ABC's *This Week*, November 19, 2006.

42. *CNN.com*, "McCain: Same-Sex Marriage Ban Is Un-Republican," July 14, 2004, www.cnn.com/2004/ALLPOLITICS/07/14/mccain.marriage.

43. Teddy Davis, "McCain Woos the Right, Makes Peace with Falwell," ABC News, March 28, 2006, http://abcnews.go.com/Politics/story?id=1779141&page=1.

44. Steve Benen, "The Old McCain Condemned Bob Jones; the New McCain . . . ," *Carpetbagger Report*, August 28, 2006, www.the carpetbaggerreport.com/archives/8313.html.

45. On the Issues, John McCain, www.ontheissues.org/John_McCain.htm#Civil_Rights.

46. John McCain addressing the South Carolina Policy Council in Charleston, South Carolina, April 20, 2000. Quoted by Steven A.

Holmes in the *New York Times,* http://query.nytimes.com/gst/fullpage
.html?res=990CE2DF1131F933A15757C0A9669C8B63..

47. Ibid.

48. Stephen A. Holmes, "After Campaigning on Candor, McCain Admits He Lacked It on Confederate Flag Issue," *New York Times,* April 20, 2000, http://query.nytimes.com/gst/fullpage.html?res=990CE2D F1131F933A15757C0A9669C8B63.

49. Ibid.

50. Max Blumenthal, "Agent of Intolerance," *The Nation,* May 16, 2007, www.thenation.com/doc/20070528/blumenthal.

51. Matt Stoller, "McCain Hires Lawbreaker as Campaign Manager," *MyDD.com,* December 7, 2006, http://www.mydd.com/ story/2006/12/7/113624/953.

CHAPTER NINE

1. See also Marjorie Cohn, *Cowboy Republic: Six Ways the Bush Gang Has Defied the Law* (Sausalito, CA: PoliPointPress, 2007).

2. Tom Curry, "Is America Turning against Wartime Measures?" MSNBC, December 15, 2005, www.msnbc.msn.com/id/10482508.

3. U.S. Senator John McCain, "McCain Urges Final Passage of the Military Commissions Act of 2006," press release, September 28, 2006, http://mccain.senate.gov/public/index.cfm?FuseAction=PressOffice .PressReleases&ContentRecord_id=4673FD86-E0C0-478D-A4E1-05F8 55E75AB5.

4. Editorial, "A Defining Moment for America," *Washington Post,* September 15, 2006, A18.

5. Ibid.

6. Associated Press, "McCain Changes Story on Tax Cut Stance," January 31, 2008, http://apnews.myway.com/article/20080131/ D8UH1CF80.html.

7. Ibid.

8. Ibid.

9. U.S. Senate Roll Call Votes 109th Congress, 2nd Session, HR 4297, Senate Vote 10, February 2, 2006, www.senate.gov/legislative/ LIS/roll_call_lists/roll_call_vote_cfm.cfm?congress=109&session=2& vote=00010.

10. Robert Novak, "John McCain: Born-Again Supply-Sider?," *Real Clear Politics*, February 5, 2007, www.realclearpolitics.com/articles/ 2007/02/john_mccain_bornagain_supplysi.html.

11. S 1415, Senate Vote 161, June 17, 1998.

12. Quoted in Chuck Collins, "War Should Be a Time of Sacrifice for Everyone," http://americansforsharedsacrifice.org/tax_cuts.htm.

13. Jim Grote, "Mt. Rushmore and a History of the Estate Tax," *Planned Giving Today*, June 2000, www.liebertpub.com/pgtoday/pgt/ articles/mt_rushmore_and_a_history.htm.

14. Ari Berman, "The Real McCain," *The Nation*, November 22, 2005, www.thenation.com/doc/20051212/berman.

15. William Brannigin, "McCain Calls to Reform Pork Barrel Politics," *Washington Post*, January 25, 2006, http://www.washington post.com/wp-dyn/content/article/2006/01/25/AR2006012501285 .html.

16. Winslow Wheeler (Spartacus), *Mr. Smith Is Dead: No One Stands in the Way as Congress Laces Post-Sept. 11 Defense Bills with Pork* (Washington, DC: World Security Institute, 2002).

17. Ibid.

18. Winslow Wheeler, interview with author, February 15, 2008.

19. Todd Purdhum, "Prisoner of Conscience," *Vanity Fair*, February 2007, www.vanityfair.com/politics/features/2007/02/mccain200702.

20. David Sirota, "World Is Flat-ism Meets the Flathead Valley," Sirotablog, December 11, 2006, http://davidsirota.com/index.php/ 2006/12/11/world-is-flat-ism-meets-the-flathead-valley.

21. News and Politics, "Best and Worst of Congress," *Washingtonian* *.com*, September 1, 2006, www.washingtonian.com/articles/media politics/1666.html.

22. Michael Shear, "Top GOP Hopefuls Keep Distance on Immigration," *Washington Post,* May 15, 2007.

23. Rick Klein, "Kennedy-McCain Partnership Falters," *Boston Globe,* March 22, 2007, www.boston.com/news/nation/washington/articles/2007/03/22/kennedy_mccain_partnership_falters/?page=2.

24. Elana Schor and Jackie Kucinich, "GOP Plots Blue-Slip Attack," *The Hill,* May 30, 2007, http://thehill.com/leading-the-news/gop-plots-blue-slip-attack-2007-05-30.html.

25. Rob Haney, interview by author, June 13, 2007.

26. Ibid.

27. Max Blumenthal, "McCain Mutiny," *The Nation,* February 21, 2007, http://www.thenation.com/doc/20070305/blumenthal.

CHAPTER TEN

1. David M. Herszenhorn, "Senate Democrats Hope for Majority Not Seen in 30 Years—60 Seats," *New York Times,* March 7, 2009.

2. Patrick McGeehan, "Texas Republican to Join UBS after He Retires from Senate," *New York Times,* October 8, 2002.

3. Michael Powell and Michael Cooper, "For Giuliani, a Dizzying Free-Fall," *New York Times,* January 30, 2008.

4. Bob Herbert, "Always Having to Say He's Sorry," *New York Times,* March 2, 2006.

5. Richard W. Stevenson, "Bush Nominates Kellogg Executive for Commerce Secretary," *New York Times,* November 30, 2004.

6. ABC, "Homeland Security Employees Rank Last in Job Satisfaction Survey," February 8, 2007, http://abclocal.go.com/wls/story?section=nation_world&id=5017688.

7. Bloomberg News, "Veto Likely for a Bill Favoring Workers," *New York Times,* November 1, 2007.

8. Juliet Eilperin, "With Talk of Cars, Romney Courts Michigan Voters," *Washington Post,* January 13, 2008.

9. Don Goldwater, in discussion with the author, June 13, 2007.

Index

national security, 26–28,
31–34. *See also* Secretary
of Homeland Security
Native Americans. *See* Indian
affairs
Naval Academy, 6–7
Nelson, Terry, 98, 121
neoconservatives (neocons),
61–62
New Jersey, 33
"No Pork Pledge," 131–32
North Korea, 75
nuclear weapons, 75, 76, 106
Nussle, Jim, 100

Obama, Barack, 44–45
Oxhorn, Liz, 29

Parsely, Rod, 107
Paxson, Lowell, 87–88
Perle, Richard, 60, 63
Perry, Bob, 92, 93
Petraeus, David, 28–29, 71
Petro, Jim, 107
Pickens, T. Boone, 93–94
Pingree, Chellie, 82
Podhoretz, Norman, 61
political action committees
(PACs), 86, 87, 95, 138
pork barrel spending, 131–33
"pork buster" speech, 132
Post-9/11 Veterans Educa-
tional Assistance Act of
2007, 37–38
Powell, Colin, 124

president, constitutional
authority of, 126–27
Project for a New American
Century, 62
Proposition 200, 137
Pryor, David, 131
Purdum, Todd, 94, 95

racial issues, 42–43, 98, 100,
118–21
racial segregation *vs.* integra-
tion, 119–21
Rassmann, Jim, 92
Reagan, Ronald, 22
Real Security Act of 2006, 31
Reid, Harry, 29
Religious Right, 1–4, 41,
105–9
Reno, Janet, 45
Renzi, Rick, 49, 95–97, 99
Reynolds, Tom, 99–100
Rhodes, Jacob, 10
Rice, Condoleezza, 141
Richards, Ann, 14
Rieckhoff, Paul, 52, 63
Robertson, Pat, 3, 4, 57, 103
Roosevelt, Theodore, 130
Rove, Karl, 62
Rumsfeld, Donald, 17, 39, 60,
62, 63, 67, 128. *See also*
Hamdan v. Rumsfeld
Russert, Tim, 18, 25, 50,
54–55

Saddam Hussein, 58–61

Acknowledgments

My first thanks must be to the late Maria Leavey, a close friend and selfless progressive hero, who told me she knew of a publisher looking for someone to write a book on John McCain and thought of me because I had been writing a lot about him. Maria was always thinking of how to help others. I wish so badly she could be here to see what she helped create.

Many others were integral to publishing this book. Chief among them is my unflappable agent, Will Lippincott, without whose advice and patience none of this ever could have happened. I am lucky to consider Will not only a first-rate representative, but also a friend. Special thanks to David Sirota for introducing us.

At PoliPointPress, my thanks go to Peter Richardson, who guided development of the book. Without his ideas, rewrites, inspiration, and occasional threats, this book probably would have lost out to a night of eight hours' sleep. Michael Coffey, whom PoliPoint brought in to help turn this book around at warp speed, has defined the word "professional" and is simply a better writer and editor than I could have ever asked to work with. Dave Peattie, Katherine Silver, and others at BookMatters provided still further polishing and, with PoliPoint's managing editor Melissa Edeburn, managed the book through prepress production in record speed.

Joe Conason, who seems to put out a bestseller every year, took time off from his busy schedule to ensure this project went forward. Bob Geiger, who helped me write parts of two chapters in this book and who is almost un-matched in his knowledge of the U.S. Senate, was also crucial to this endeavor. Bob Grossfeld, the uber-talented media consultant from Arizona, has also been essential. Bob introduced me to many of the players in McCain's home state.

Thank you to Robert Greenwald for joining with me to start therealmccain.com and for giving me an outlet to explore the good senator online. And to those who took hours helping me edit the book—including John Ehrenfeld, Paddy Kraska, Dave Riegel, and some fantasti-cally talented woman named Anne Luecke—my gratitude is boundless.

Along the way, numerous friends and associates gave me encouragement; I wish I could thank them all here. Some went beyond a "go get 'em" to significantly help my career or to give me advice, leads, or funding for this book. So thank you Hebah Abdella, Peggy Albrecht, John Amato, Phillip Anderson, John Aravosis, Ira Arlook, Matt Bailey, Nicole Belle, Duncan Black, Becky Bond,

Randy Borntrager, Wes Boyd, Matt Browner-Hamlin, Mike Casey, Bob Cesca, Nita Chaudhary, Peter B. Collins, Tula Connell, Brett Di Resta, Charlie Fink, Trevor Fitzgibbon, Robert Fox, Judith Freeman, Valerie French, Jim Gilliam, Joshua Glasstetter, John Gorenfeld, Bob Griffith, Matt Gross, David Grossman, Jane Hamsher, Diane Hodges, Jerome Hohman, Joshua Holland, Eileen Holloway, Rick Jacobs, Jordan Karp, Sean-Paul Kelley, Howie Klein, Alan Kraut, Justin Krebs, Peter Kuznick, Kombiz Lavasany, Judd Legum, Jared Leopold, Andrew Lewis, Allan Lichtman, Steve Lubot, Marilyn Luecke, Dan Manatt, Arnie Mazer, Bill Mazer, Jennifer Nix, Karen Nussbaum, Eli Pariser, Rick Perlstein, Nico Pitney, Sarah Posner, Ari Rabin-Havt, Todd Robinson, Mike Rogers, Brian Rothenberg, Bob Ruth, Tom Schaller, Bill Scher, Sam Seder, John Shay, Mike Stark, Colin Sterling, Matt Stoller, Lee Stranahan, Jeff Tiedrich, Mike Tomasky, Joe Trippi, Cenk Uygur, Paul Waldman, Joel Wright, and Murshed Zaheed.

Thank you to everybody who took time out of their busy days to provide interviews and enlighten this poor misguided soul on many important issues: Steve Benen, Ari Berman, Chris Bowers, Leonard Clark, William Crum, Joe Gigante, Don Goldwater, Glenn Greenwald, Paul Hackett, Rob Haney, Christy Hardin Smith, Jack Hitt, Larry Johnson, David Neiwert, Russell Pearce, Paul Rieckhoff, Chris Simcox, Jonathan Singer, Joe Sudbay, Lyle Tuttle, Richard Viguerie, and Winslow Wheeler.

As I have most certainly forgotten some people, let me apologize to anyone I have missed. Some of the unnamed are not forgotten. Thank you to the many brave souls who spoke honestly with me off the record. What you told me helped shape this book in ways otherwise impossible. In any cases in which your intentions remained in doubt, I have purposefully left you out—so please know that even though you don't appear here, you have my eternal thanks.

Finally, thanks to the Republican presidential candidates for running such bad campaigns. Fred Thompson, Rudy Giuliani, and Mitt Romney deserve special mention here. Had any of you come close to living up to expectations, this book would have remained a shelved, six-month waste of my time and money. You guys are the best!

CLIFF SCHECTER is a political consultant and commentator for National Public Radio, MSNBC, CNN, and Fox News. He is a frequent contributor to the *Huffington Post*, Air America, the *Guardian Online*, Americablog, and *The Young Turks*, the first nationwide liberal talk show and first live, daily internet TV show. He lectures on American politics at the U.S. State Department's Bureau of International Information Programs and is a senior fellow at Working America (a division of the AFL-CIO) and Progress Ohio. He is CEO and president of the Lucky Media Group, LLC, which provides media advice to progressive entities and candidates.

OTHER BOOKS FROM POLIPOINTPRESS

The Blue Pages: A Directory of Companies Rated by Their Politics and Practices
Helps consumers match their buying decisions with their political values by listing the political contributions and business practices of over 1,000 companies. $9.95, paperback.

Jeff Cohen, Cable News Confidential: My Misadventures in Corporate Media
Offers a fast-paced romp through the three major cable news channels—Fox CNN, and MSNBC—and delivers a serious message about their failure to cover the most urgent issues of the day. $14.95, paperback.

Marjorie Cohn, Cowboy Republic: Six Ways the Bush Gang Has Defied the Law
Shows how the executive branch under President Bush has systematically defied the law instead of enforcing it. $14.95, paperback.

Joe Conason, The Raw Deal: How the Bush Republicans Plan to Destroy Social Security and the Legacy of the New Deal
Reveals the well-financed and determined effort to undo the Social Security Act and other New Deal programs. $11.00, paperback.

Kevin Danaher, Shannon Biggs, and Jason Mark, Building the Green Economy: Success Stories from the Grassroots
Shows how community groups, families, and individual citizens have protected their food and water, cleaned up their neighborhoods, and strengthened their local economies. $16.00, paperback.

Reese Erlich, The Iran Agenda: The Real Story of U.S. Policy and the Middle East Crisis
Explores the turbulent recent history between the two countries and how it has led to a showdown over nuclear technology. $14.95, paperback.

Steven Hill, *10 Steps to Repair American Democracy*
Identifies the key problems with American democracy, especially election practices, and proposes ten specific reforms to reinvigorate it. $11.00, paperback.

Markos Kounalakis and Peter Laufer, *Hope Is a Tattered Flag: Voices of Reason and Change for the Post-Bush Era*
Gathers together the most listened-to politicos and pundits, activists and thinkers, to answer the question: what happens after Bush leaves office? $29.95, hardcover; $16.95 paperback.

Yvonne Latty, *In Conflict: Iraq War Veterans Speak Out on Duty, Loss, and the Fight to Stay Alive*
Features the unheard voices, extraordinary experiences, and personal photographs of a broad mix of Iraq War veterans, including Congressman Patrick Murphy, Tammy Duckworth, Kelly Daugherty, and Camilo Mejia. $24.00, hardcover.

Phillip Longman, *Best Care Anywhere: Why VA Health Care Is Better Than Yours*
Shows how the turnaround at the long-maligned VA hospitals provides a blueprint for salvaging America's expensive but troubled health care system. $14.95, paperback.

Susan Mulcahy, ed., *Why I'm a Democrat*
Explores the values and passions that make a diverse group of Americans proud to be Democrats. $14.95, paperback.

Christine Pelosi, *Campaign Boot Camp: Basic Training for Future Leaders*
Offers a seven-step guide for successful campaigns and causes at all levels of government. $15.95, paperback.

William Rivers Pitt, *House of Ill Repute: Reflections on War, Lies, and America's Ravaged Reputation*
Skewers the Bush Administration for its reckless invasions, warrantless wiretaps, lethally incompetent response to Hurricane Katrina, and other scandals and blunders. $16.00, paperback.

Sarah Posner, *God's Profits: Faith, Fraud, and the Republican Crusade for Values Voters*
Examines corrupt televangelists' ties to the Republican Party and unprecedented access to the Bush White House. $19.95, hardcover.

Nomi Prins, *Jacked: How "Conservatives" Are Picking Your Pocket –Whether You Voted for Them or Not*
Describes how the "conservative" agenda has affected your wallet, skewed national priorities, and diminished America—but not the American spirit. $12.00, paperback.

Norman Solomon, *Made Love, Got War: Close Encounters with America's Warfare State*
Traces five decades of American militarism and the media's all-too-frequent failure to challenge it. $24.95, hardcover.

John Sperling et al., *The Great Divide: Retro vs. Metro America*
Explains how and why our nation is so bitterly divided into what the authors call Retro and Metro America. $19.95, paperback.

Daniel Weintraub, *Party of One: Arnold Schwarzenegger and the Rise of the Independent Voter*
Explains how Schwarzenegger found favor with independent voters, whose support has been critical to his success, and suggests that his bipartisan approach represents the future of American politics. $19.95, hardcover.

Curtis White, *The Spirit of Disobedience: Resisting the Charms of Fake Politics, Mindless Consumption, and the Culture of Total Work*
Debunks the notion that liberalism has no need for spirituality and describes a "middle way" through our red state/blue state political impasse. Includes three powerful interviews with John DeGraaf, James Howard Kunstler, and Michael Ableman. $24.00, hardcover.

FOR MORE INFORMATION, PLEASE VISIT WWW.P3BOOKS.COM.

ABOUT THIS BOOK

This book is printed on Cascade Enviro100 Print paper. It contains 100 percent post-consumer fiber and is certified EcoLogo, Processed Chlorine Free, and FSC Recycled. For each ton used instead of virgin paper, we:

- Save the equivalent of 17 trees
- Reduce air emissions by 2,098 pounds
- Reduce solid waste by 1,081 pounds
- Reduce the water used by 10,196 gallons
- Reduce suspended particles in the water by 6.9 pounds.

This paper is manufactured using biogas energy, reducing natural gas consumption by 2,748 cubic feet per ton of paper produced.

The book's printer, Malloy Incorporated, works with paper mills that are environmentally responsible, that do not source fiber from endangered forests, and that are third-party certified. Malloy prints with soy- and vegetable-based inks, and more than 98 percent of the solid material they discard is recycled. Their water emissions are entirely safe for disposal into their municipal sanitary sewer system, and they work with the Michigan Department of Environmental Quality to ensure that their air emissions meet all environmental standards.

The Michigan Department of Environmental Quality has recognized Malloy as a Great Printer for their compliance with environmental regulations, written environmental policy, pollution prevention efforts, and a pledge to share best practices with other printers. Their county Department of Planning and Environment has designated them a Waste Knot Partner for their waste prevention and recycling programs.